Love &
Mom

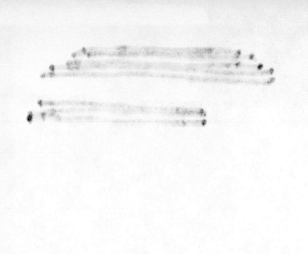

Project Management
for Small Design Firms

Other McGraw-Hill Books of Interest

Project Management for Small Design Firms

Howard G. Birnberg
Birnberg & Associates
Chicago, Illinois

McGraw-Hill, Inc.
New York St. Louis San Francisco Auckland Bogotá
Caracas Lisbon London Madrid Mexico Milan
Montreal New Delhi Paris San Juan São Paulo
Singapore Sydney Tokyo Toronto

Library of Congress Cataloging-in-Publication Data

Birnberg, Howard G.
    Project management for small design firms / Howard G. Birnberg
        p.   cm.
    Includes bibliographical references and index.
    ISBN 0-07-005400-2
    1. Architectural firms—United States—Management.   2. Engineering
firms—United States—Management.   I. Title.
    NA1996.B5   1992
    720′.68—dc20   92-6393
                                                               CIP

1 2 3 4 5 6 7 8 9 0   DOC/DOC   9 8 7 6 5 4 3 2

ISBN   0-07-005400-2

*The sponsoring editor for this book was Joel Stein, the editing
supervisor was Mitsy Kovacs, and the production supervisor was
Donald Schmidt. This book was set in Century Schoolbook by
McGraw-Hill's Professional Book Group composition unit.*

Printed and bound by R. R. Donnelley & Sons Company.

*To Diane Mix Birnberg and
Michael Samuel Birnberg*

Contents

Part 4   Managing the Project

Preface

The fundamental element of a design firm is its project management system. This system enables firms to successfully complete projects and hence solve their clients' problems. The project is the profit center of the organization. The individual who manages the project, the project manager, is in the best position to control the final outcome of a job and can have a great effect on project and firm profitability. However, not all project managers function in the same manner. Many firms have what is known as a weak project management system. Typically, in this type of system the principal or partner is responsible for client contact while the project manager is responsible for actually producing the work. In effect, the project manager is really a technician.

I have often heard practitioners say that profitability and growth are factors in the ability to "get the work" (that is, in the success of the marketing effort). I believe that this is only partially true. A much more fundamental factor is the firm's project management system. With a strong project management system, the principals can and should spend more effort getting the work and managing the firm.

Many firms pride themselves on personal service to the client. However, with a weak or ineffective project management system, the principal often deals with the client, and the project manager is in charge of producing the work. However, no one individual has complete control of the project, hence efficiency and profitability suffer. In essence, when more than one individual is responsible for the project, in reality no one is. As a result, the desired personal service is often a myth because those who are actually responsible for performing the work rarely communicate directly with the client.

In small firms the failure of the project management system can be disastrous. Significantly exceeding the budget or schedule on even one major job can lead to a financial loss for the year for the practice, or even worse consequences.

Doubling up of job responsibilities requires tight control and effective planning. Principals must strike a proper balance between firm management and project management. The lack of staff to fully develop a strong project management system is no excuse. Many of the forms, checklists, and procedures described in this book apply equally to design firms of all sizes.

What Is a Small Design Firm?

There is no universal agreement on the definition of a small design firm. The American Institute of Architects publishes a biennial *Architecture Factbook*. In recent years, approximately 83 percent of AIA member firms had a total staff of nine members or less. According to the American Consulting Engineers Council, the median total staff size of its member firms is about six or seven.

Small staff size does not mean that a design firm's capabilities must be limited. Being small is more a state of mind than a real limit on a firm's ability to be well-managed, competitive, and profitable. When reviewing the material in this book, look for ways you can apply it to your firm and always strive for better project management.

Acknowledgments

The author would like to thank the following for their assistance and contributions to this book:

Thomas Eyerman, FAIA, for the material on networking in Chap. 11. Mr. Eyerman, former partner in charge of finance and administration of Skidmore, Owings & Merrill, 1968-1990, is now concentrating on service to professional firms as an independent advisor and counselor. He is founder of Delphi Associates Ltd.

Lowell V. Getz, CPA, for the material on contract types in Chap. 14. Mr. Getz regularly consults on design firm valuation and ownership transition.

Gene Montgomery, AIA, for the material on project administration in Chap. 14, much of Chap. 17 except for "Billing Clients for CADD," and all of Chap. 18. He is a principal of Jack Train Associates, Chicago.

Jeffrey Orlove, AIA, for the section "Developing a Quality Assurance Program" in Chap. 16. Mr. Orlove is executive vice president and principal in charge of management for the Chicago-based architectural, planning, and interior design firm of Solomon Cordwell Buenz and Associates, Inc.

John Schlossman, FAIA, for "Peer Review: Help or Heartburn?" in Chap. 16. Mr. Schlossman is a principal of the Chicago-based architectural firm of Loebl, Schlossman & Hackl. He is a former member of the National AIA Liability Committee.

Sabine Champagne (Northwestern University, Medill School of Journalism, Class of 1993) for editing the manuscript and word processing.

Bonnie Pendlebury for endless hours of word processing.

Howard Birnberg

Project Management
for Small Design Firms

Organizing for Project Management

Chapter

1

The Need for
Project Management

Effective project management is important to all design firms. Small firms are especially handicapped by a lack of project control and reporting systems, a lack of staff time solely devoted to managing projects, insufficient principal time to run both the firm and projects, and an inability to market with enough regularity to ensure a steady work load.

In addition, many smaller practices find it difficult to apply published or seminar material on project management. The situations described often assume necessary staff and resources to implement prescribed systems and practices. In the typical small firm, principals run projects and the firm. They make all decisions (major and minor), work on the boards, meet with clients, keep project and financial records, negotiate contracts and become involved in dozens of other tasks on a daily basis. Many of these individuals find it difficult to understand how project management techniques designed for larger firms are relevant to their situation.

There are, however, many excellent procedures appropriate for large and small design firms that enable firms to escape the treadmill of constant crisis management. Systems and methods can be implemented that will make design practice more efficient and profitable. For example, firms with shorter-duration projects may want to selectively incorporate project management techniques based on the specific situations presented. It may not, for example, be sensible to establish an elaborate project status reporting system for projects whose duration may be measured in days, not months or even weeks. In this case, the system may not be current enough to allow the principals or project manager to take corrective action in the event of problems.

The reporting system should, however, provide enough information to record historical data on project profitability, change orders required, basic contract terms, and similar information.

Every firm should use a personal computer to do word processing and maintain basic project cost and financial records and billing information. Checklists should be used for project control and should not be left to individual memory. The goal of small-firm project management is to save time, cut costs, and increase productivity and profitability.

Project Management Problems

All design firms have their own project management problems. A recent survey by Birnberg & Associates of 110 design practices compiled a list of the most significant project problems affecting them. Dozens of items were listed, and some responses were unclear as to the exact nature of the problem. But there were a number of problems listed repeatedly. In a class by itself was the difficulty of making a profit and staying within the budget. Clearly, these are goals of any project management system. Design firms have a long way to go to achieve them.

With multiple answers, the number of mentions shown in Table 1.1 will be more than the total number of respondents. Percentages indicate total respondents mentioning this item.

Other problems noted but not shown include: personnel planning (3), contractors (3), project closeout (3), and timely decision making

TABLE 1.1   Project Management Problems

Problem	Mentions	Percent
Making a profit/budgets	34	30.9
Meeting schedules and deadlines	18	16.4
Change-order and/or scope management	17	15.5
Internal communications	16	14.5
Quality control	14	12.7
Client communications	13	11.8
Lack of experienced staff and/or PMs	12	10.9
Low fees/determining fees	9	8.2
Planning/scheduling work	9	8.2
Time management	9	8.2
Poor marketing/uneven work load	7	6.4
Salaries/personnel issues	6	5.5
Billing and collection	4	3.6
Consultants	4	3.6
Poor cost accounting	4	3.6
Project documentation	4	3.6

(2). No design firm can ever hope to avoid all of these problems, but a strong project management system can help minimize many of them.

Design Firm Life Cycle Curve

Few principals objectively evaluate the patterns of growth and stagnation in their firms. Through research data assembled from design firm financial surveys and other sources, a profile of the typical life cycle of a design practice has been developed.

The vertical axis in Fig. 1.1 measures common values of growth—typically, fee levels, profits, staff size, etc. Although these are the most common measures, others should not be excluded if they are appropriate for your firm (productivity per staff member, number of offices, etc.). The horizontal axis measures the number of years of the firm's existence. There are no ideal points or values for each phase, since the specific levels are only important as they reflect *your* ability to adapt as your firm grows, stagnates, or declines. *Understanding the curve, the triggers to growth, and the causes of stagnation and decline are the important concepts.*

Phase 1: Organization

Most design firms begin with the founder(s) breaking away from an established practice with one or more initial clients. Often, a firm will begin with 6- to 8-month backlog of work. Unfortunately, because marketing is rarely a major part of an individual's responsibility at the former firm, skills in obtaining additional projects are often lacking. Most firms stay small because many principals cannot solve the dilemma of how to do the work and still manage and market. As a result, most principals neglect management and marketing until a crisis occurs—they run out of work.

A small percentage of the firms grow out of the organizational phase of the life cycle by early development of fundamental marketing

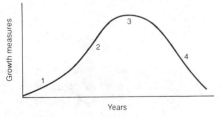

Figure 1.1 Life cycle curve.

and management systems and procedures. Often, these firms rely on having an interested, effective marketer and a project management system.

Phase 2: Growth

For a great many firms, rapid growth occurs because of the ability of one or two individuals in the firm to intuitively market. Often, one large project or client will trigger a cycle of rapid expansion. This growth occurs for 4 or 5 years and is followed by a period of temporary or permanent stagnation. Usually high-growth firms quickly outgrow the systems and processes established during the organizational phase, and attempts to cope with growth often result in patchwork solutions.

For most firms in the growth phase, the following is typical:

- Senior managers' management style is slow to change even as conditions change.
- Middle managers are often given responsibility without corresponding authority.
- Management and marketing experience is lacking at all levels of the firm's management and is often obtained only after growth has been hindered by poor performance.
- Significant communication problems develop internally and with clients.

To avoid stagnation, systems and management approach must adapt. Senior-level managers must devote time and resources to planning, organizing, and marketing.

Phase 3: Stagnation

The first sign of creeping stagnation is marked by stagnating or declining levels of profit even as the firm increases fees or staff size. Profits decline because of soaring overhead brought on by low productivity and ineffective operations. For some firms, stagnation may be initially caused by the loss of a major client, or by key middle or senior managers who leave the firm to begin their own practices (and repeat many of the same mistakes).

Short-term stagnation can be beneficial as a time of consolidation and reorganization; prolonged stagnation (3 to 5 years or more) can be dangerous. Firms deeply into the stagnation phase find themselves losing old clients to other design firms and find old management and marketing systems breaking down or becoming ineffective for a changing marketplace. In some firms, senior principals create a stagnant situation as they grow tired or disinterested in the practice. Without some change, decline is inevitable. Change can mean selling ownership to young managers, merging with another firm, computerizing effectively, developing aggressive marketing, etc. Prolonged stagnation will be fatal to any design practice.

Phase 4: Decline

The decline phase of the life-cycle curve is a direct result of unarrested stagnation brought on by a continued loss of repeat clients and key staff. The decline phase is marked by an extended period of financial losses resulting in severe cash flow difficulties. Bank borrowings often become extensive in an effort to finance continued operations. An aging staff and leadership becomes increasingly inbred and ineffective.

For many firms, the decline continues as long as a principal remains with the practice. Eventually, a critical point is reached where the firm cannot be saved except by a sellout or a merger using any remaining assets, contracts, or staff. Often, on the death, illness, or retirement of the last principal, the firm ceases to exist.

It is impossible to generalize a firm's life-cycle curve from only a few years' experience. There will always be short-term ups and downs because of fluctuations in the economy, sudden loss of a major client, or the illness of a key staff member or manager. However, over a period of years, nearly all firms will experience a pattern similar to the life-cycle curve outlined here. Well-managed firms look for controlled, planned growth and continually conduct long-range planning, marketing planning, staff and management training, and conduct regular self-analysis sessions.

2

Project Delivery System

System Types

There are as many methods of organizing for project delivery as there are design firms. Most well-managed firms are forever tinkering with their systems in an effort to improve service to their clients and their own profitability. Some firms even use different systems within their operation, depending on the project size, location, client need, and other factors. However, these systems generally fall into one of three formats.

Pyramid Approach

This method revolves around a key individual who makes all major (and often minor) decisions (see Fig. 2.1). It is commonly used in smaller firms where the firm's owner has daily involvement in all project and firm management decisions. One or more key technical and administrative support people aid in executing required tasks. Lower-level staff members generally perform only assigned tasks. If

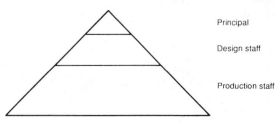

Principal

Design staff

Production staff

Figure 2.1 Pyramid Approach.

the key individual is not available, activity often grinds to a halt. In a busy firm, daily crisis management may rule, and important issues, such as short- and long-term marketing, may be neglected.

Where a firm has two or more partners, multiple pyramids may exist. Each partner may have his or her own group of clients and key technical assistant. Formal coordination between partners rarely exists, and important planning issues are usually neglected. Where one principal is more successful in obtaining work, his or her share of the firm's work load may become overwhelming. This often creates friction and conflict between partners.

Some firms deal with these problems by organizing an informal division of labor, whereby assigned project and administrative roles are given to each principal. Unfortunately, most principals still prefer project involvement and continue to neglect their assigned administrative or marketing functions.

In some larger firms a studio approach is used that resembles the pyramid in Fig. 2.1. A studio is the permanent establishment of a team or teams, many of whom specialize in certain types of projects (e.g., medical facilities studio, educational facilities studio). These teams handle projects of various sizes and use floaters who are assigned to a studio team as additional help is needed. Each studio may have senior designers, production supervisor, technicians, researchers, drafters, specifiers, and observers. The concept is similar to having a series of small offices within a large one.

Departmental Organization

As firms grow, pressure increases to formalize project and nonproject management assignments. The division-of-labor concept often becomes the basis for a formal departmental structure. For example, a single-discipline firm often structures itself around marketing, design, production, and field departments. Multidisciplinary firms may establish each discipline as a separate department (Fig. 2.2).

Single-discipline firms frequently appoint department heads drawn from associate or principal ranks. These individuals normally retain full authority for all project and nonproject decision making within their departments. Responsibility for project management is usually

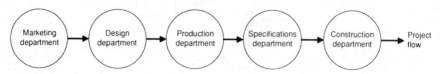

Figure 2.2   Departmental organization.

delegated to the next lower staff level, and these individuals are called *project managers* or *project engineers* or *architects*.

The concept behind the departmental approach holds that, as one department completes its work on time, within the budget and according to the contractual scope, project authority and responsibility are passed to the next department head or through the designated manager within the department.

In reality, department heads base their project priorities on their own work load, level of interest in the project, relationship with the client, and other factors. Often, each department and its head have different methods of project management and capabilities. As a result, clients must adjust their operation to three or more different project styles and systems. In addition, if the firm's principals assume departmental responsibilities, firm management and marketing may still be neglected. Under the single-discipline departmental organization, the situation may be little improved over the pyramid approach, since each department may simply become its own pyramid. With no one individual in charge of the entire project, personal service to the client is often a myth, and time schedules, budgets, profits, and the long-term well-being of the firm may all be jeopardized.

In an attempt to deal with the deficiencies of the single-discipline departmental system, some firms have introduced the project manager concept. Unfortunately, this system is not designed or operated properly by most firms. All too often, firms institute a weak project management system where there is a significant imbalance between responsibility and authority. To be successful, levels of responsibility must be generally equal to levels of authority. In many firms, real decision-making authority remains with department heads, while much of the project responsibility is delegated to project managers. As a result, project managers lack the authority, training, or experience to make decisions stick, and simply cease being decision makers. This discredits the project manager and management systems in the eyes of department heads, senior managers, and clients. Where department heads are generally owners and project managers are associates or employees, the situation may become intolerable. In these firms, staff turnover may be high, profitability and productivity low, and client satisfaction questionable.

Multidiscipline firms can successfully use a departmental approach when most projects are within a single discipline. Often, these firms establish a matrix management system within each department. Where studios are used, a similar system may be developed.

Multidisciplinary firms with projects involving several disciplines require a project management system to handle work that crosses department lines. Often, a project manager is selected according to the predominant discipline required. Without an effective project manager, multidisciplinary firms may find themselves with the same problems as single-discipline, departmentally organized firms.

Matrix Management

For many design firms, the matrix management (or strong project manager) approach functions best (Fig. 2.3). Under this system the project manager is in full charge of the project from beginning (marketing) to end (continued contact). The project manager has an equal balance of authority and responsibility and is the firm's primary client contact point. The project manager's major responsibilities include meeting the client's program and budget while maintaining profitability for the firm. Department heads or chiefs of the various functional areas (marketing, design, production, etc.) retain responsibility and authority for technical decisions, staff assignments, training in technical areas, implementing quality control reviews, etc. Where technical decisions significantly affect the project scope or budget, the project manager (and often the client) must review and approve decisions.

The matrix project management system separates the ownership role from the need to produce a successful and profitable project for both the client and the firm. Unfortunately, at times of conflict, there is a tendency to confuse ownership with a project's real needs.

To be successful, a firm using the matrix management system must be able to communicate to its staff and client how the system works. On occasion, confusion can arise on the part of staff members regarding who to contact with questions, comments, or problems (the project manager or a department/functional head). In addition, matrix man-

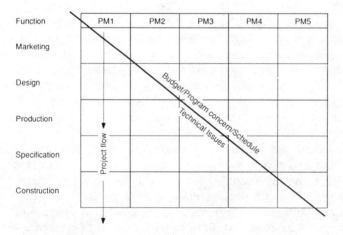

Figure 2.3 Strong project manager matrix.

agement requires a complete, timely, and accurate job cost reporting system. Other management tools such as a project management manual are also extremely helpful.

Small firms, or large firms with small projects, may establish an abbreviated matrix system. In this case, an individual may wear several hats and must be careful to focus on specific responsibilities on a project. Some firms use the full matrix system only on their larger projects and use other approaches on their remaining jobs.

The matrix system requires a strong chief executive to arbitrate disputes between project managers, department/functional heads, and staff members. Although the goal of the system is to avoid bottlenecks and crisis management, disputes will occur, and these require careful resolution. When functioning properly, matrix systems encourage decision making at the lowest effective level of the organization, and both responsibility and authority must be delegated to make this possible.

The Project Manager

3

Who Is a Project Manager?

A survey conducted by the Association for Project Managers (APM) shows that design firms have vastly different definitions of the role of the project manager. Most, however, claim that many or all of their jobs are managed by a project manager (PM). More than 80 percent indicated that their projects are managed by an individual with the title of project manager.

About 55 percent of the firms surveyed had four project managers or fewer. The mean (average) number of PMs when all firms were included in the survey was 6.5. Finding and keeping capable project managers remains a vexing problem for many design firms. Nearly one-third (30.8 percent) of the respondents reported difficulty in hiring and retaining managers. Turnover in the PM ranks is another significant problem, with nearly 45 percent of firms suffering some loss in the ranks of these key individuals in a 1-year period. Table 3.1 highlights this finding.

In many design firms, principals often assume project management responsibilities. For small practices this is necessary because of the

TABLE 3.1 Number of PMs Leaving During the Past Year

Number	Frequency	Percent
0	60	56.6
1	28	26.4
2	12	11.4
3	3	2.8
4 or more	3	2.8
	106	100.0
Missing = 4		

lack of sufficient staff to serve as project managers. In other cases, it is the principal's preference to undertake project management in addition to other firm management and marketing responsibilities.

The survey found that 85 percent of the firms' principals assume some or all project management activities. The average number of principals per firm handling PM work was nearly two. This finding is particularly significant when the average number of principals per firm was found to be only 2.7.

Project managers tend to be among the most highly experienced individuals in design firms. The mean number of years of professional experience for PMs was 9.7 and the median was 8.5. The range was from 1 to 44 years.

Characteristics of Project Managers

The greatest need in many design firms is for skilled project managers. Few university curriculums provide even rudimentary management training. Necessary project management skills are learned on the job or through seminars or self-initiative. Most designers have little ability or interest in the business side of architecture or engineering. Often, those who show even the slightest inclination toward management are pushed to become project managers. In some firms, however, the best technicians are "made" project managers on the basis of their proven ability in a chosen area.

Who should be a project manager? How are they created? What characteristics are important? No one would dispute the fact that the best technicians often make the poorest project managers. The reason for this is obvious. Most individuals with a proven technical ability tend to focus strongly on the aspect of the project with greatest interest to them. With few exceptions, this focus works to the detriment of the broader project needs that a project manager must address. Clearly, it is the best all-around manager who is the ideal project manager. But, what capabilities should this individual possess?

Strong organizational ability

The successful project manager must be able to organize a project and the team and address the many details that arise. The PM must be strong at organizing personnel schedules and be able to handle more than one major project if necessary.

Generalist

While managers may have an interest in a particular project area, they must be familiar with all aspects of the project. However, project managers do not need to know all of the technical details for themselves. Being an effective delegator is very important.

Insight

To be effective as a project manager, one must have a strong ability to examine the broad scope of a client's problem without becoming bogged down in details.

Ability to monitor the project

A project manager must be able to monitor project status and display a willingness to ask for assistance when the situation warrants. Effective communications between members of the project team is vital.

Communicative

Project managers must have good communications skills for both speaking and writing. They must be able to communicate to both individuals and groups as marketers and as managers of the project team. In addition, they must be good listeners.

Presentable

Personal appearance and professionalism must be maintained at a very high level, since the project manager is the firm's primary representative to the client. The manager is a public person and must have high regard for the firm's image.

Experience

Successful project managers must have broad experience in a variety of building types. They must have strong skills and experience in project budgeting, negotiating, marketing, and estimating. They should also have their own database of previous project experiences.

Leadership ability

The strong project manager must be a leader; an individual who can direct and motivate the team. The PM should have demonstrated leadership ability prior to becoming a project manager.

Ability to make decisions

A project manager is a decision maker. The ability to make decisions and to carry them through is vital. In addition, the manager must be able to admit a mistake and to say no to a client or staff member when necessary.

In general, most of the qualities and characteristics of the successful project manager revolve around the ability to work well with people, rather than technical abilities. Certainly, the PM must have basic technical skills, but overemphasis on these by senior management will not necessarily result in a good project manager. All project managers require regular training to improve skills and to learn new ones. This training must become a regular part of creating project managers.

4

Project Managers' Responsibilities

One of the emerging trends in design firms is a renewed focus on project management. Gone are the days when any firm could afford poor project management practices. Fewer projects and tighter budgets are forcing design firm managers to make significant changes in their operations.

If this is to be the era of the project manager, there are specific areas which require design firm attention.

Areas Requiring Attention

Organization

In recent years, many designers have established project management systems. Unfortunately, most of them have a weak version of this system. While project managers may have been appointed, principals and other senior managers are often slow to give up control over projects. As a result, project managers have titles and responsibilities, but they lack the effective authority to make decisions stick.

For firms to be successful at project management, a true delegation of responsibility and authority must occur. Greater education on the role of project management in design firms is also required. Principals must understand the strong project management system and the role of the individual project manager.

Recruiting

Project management requires a unique set of skills often lacking in technically trained individuals. Many firms lack a clear idea of the role of the project manager. As a result, they are uncertain as to the necessary skills. As noted in Chap. 3, some firms still select project managers for their technical expertise, not on their leadership and management skills.

Many well-managed companies establish career tracks for their employees. This may include a design, technical, or management track. Position descriptions are clearly written, organizational structure is established, and individuals are recruited or promoted to fill a defined need.

Training

Few firms have adequate training programs. This lack of training strongly affects project managers who require the broadest range of skills of any design firm member.

A good training program will have these areas of focus:

1. Training staff in the firm's methods of operation
2. Providing replacements and support for existing staff
3. Improving job performance and productivity

For many design firms developing a project management system, an individual experienced in project management must be hired to guide the effort. Often, this individual brings to the firm an understanding of how the system should function and may bring forms, checklists, procedures, etc. that can speed up the implementation process. This manager often provides initial training to other project managers.

Productivity

The years ahead will continue to require enhanced focus on how to improve productivity. Computer-aided design and drafting (CADD) and computers can be of great help. Unfortunately, they can significantly change a firm's work methods and can require totally new approaches to producing drawings. Project managers must be aware of these changes or productivity will actually be diminished.

Specialization can affect firm productivity and may require project managers who are experts in a particular type of work. Providing the necessary tools and information to these key individuals will allow them to improve job performance and will enhance productivity.

Project Manager Responsibilities

There are as many definitions of a project manager's responsibilities as there are design firms. In some firms, a project manager is anyone who tells someone else what to do. In one extreme case, a 50-person architectural practice claimed that 20 people were project managers.

There is no viable rule of thumb for the number of project managers needed for a certain number of jobs. However, where a full-charge project manager runs the job with the proper tools and staff, a large number of projects can be managed by one individual.

The following is a list of some of the major responsibilities of PMs. Clearly, this is not a complete list, so firms developing a project manager position description should seek additional resources. (See "Example Outline for the Project Manager's Manual," p. 36.)

Marketing and continued contact

Most experienced clients want to meet with and discuss their project with the individual actually responsible for the job. Initial contact and discussions should be held with the marketing staff or principal; however, the project manager should be brought into the process as soon as possible.

The PM should also function as a source of continuing contact with clients on completed projects. This will ensure the smooth functioning of the facility and keep the firm aware of further services required by the client.

Proposal preparation and fee determination and negotiation

One of the most important responsibilities of project managers is preparing a proposed scope of services and determining the corresponding fee. As the individual responsible for meeting the scope and fee, the PM must buy into them. Scopes and fees imposed by senior management will not allow for full accountability. With less experienced managers, a thorough review process is essential.

While final contract signing must be done by a representative of the ownership of the design firm, the project manager should lead the fee- and scope-negotiating process. This provides for full accountability in the event adjustments in scope or fee are required.

Personnel planning and assembly of the project team

The project manager is closest to the project and the required personnel needs and schedule. The PM must provide regular input to senior management to allow planning of overall firm personnel needs.

As the project begins, the PM must suggest names of specific individuals who should work on the job. This is based upon the PM's knowledge of the needs of the project and the specific skills of staff members. Obviously, the suggested list must be adjusted according to other projects' needs and the availability of various individuals.

Managing the project

The project manager is responsible for supervising all phases of the project, including time charges, meeting budgets (both fee and construction) and handling the many other details of guiding a project through the office. While most project managers should not be making technical or design decisions, in some cases this becomes necessary to ensure compliance with the program.

Quality control

Quality control is a shared responsibility. However, the PM must ensure that quality control reviews are budgeted for in the project fee and take place at the appropriate time. In some firms, where the PMs have the technical competence, they may actually red-line drawings themselves.

It is the responsibility of senior management to develop a quality assurance program. The technical staff and the project managers must ensure that the program is instituted.

Client relations

It is the project manager who can best communicate with the client. There must be a regular process of meetings, telephone calls, and correspondence. The specific and implied needs of the client must be clearly understood by the PM. Managers must control change orders and out-of-scope items by developing a regular process to inform clients of the status of these items.

Project status reporting

A project manager must not only prepare an original project budget, but must also feed the reporting system by providing accurate budgets, contract data, percentages of completion, etc. on a timely basis. Information including revised budgets and maximums on change orders must also be kept current. Project status reports must be closely monitored and PMs must address problems before they become crises.

Billing and collection

Although in most firms invoices are prepared by the accounting office, the project manager should review and approve all invoices prior to issuance to clients. The PM should not be responsible for collecting invoices, but, with a close relationship with the client, may be able to expedite collections.

Project Managers and Marketing

Project managers can and should have a major role in a design firm's marketing effort. Unfortunately, many practices fail to properly integrate their project managers into the marketing team. This failure can seriously affect the marketing success rate and future project profitability. Well-managed organizations train their project managers to have a key function in marketing.

To be effective in the marketing effort, project managers should:

1. *Be assigned to a particular potential project at an early stage.* Once it has been determined that a lead is materializing into a tangible project opportunity, a project manager should be assigned. The PM should participate in subsequent marketing activities and later manage the project if the effort is successful.

2. *Serve as a primary contact person for the future client.* This role is shared with the senior marketer. The project manager must be the client's point of contact on technical and scope issues while the senior marketer/principal is the liaison on other issues. Clearly, the project manager and marketers must meet regularly and maintain a healthy communication.

3. *Provide technical input to both the marketing staff and the future client.* This role may include assistance in the preparation of a preliminary project program or the suggesting of alternatives that may have lower initial or life-cycle cost, allow for easier expansion, etc. As a result of this effort, firm members may demonstrate their experience, knowledge, and strong concern for the future client's needs and budget.

4. *Participate in the presentation process.* Most experienced clients want to meet the individual who will be responsible for managing and performing the work. The presentation process is an ideal time to involve the project manager with the future client because it allows the project manager to provide specific information as to how the project will be managed. It also helps to establish a good working relationship with the client. The project manager should have an active role in preparing materials and strategies for presentations.

5. *Develop a detailed project scope.* Clearly, the project manager has far more experience than most other marketers in the development of the project scope. With early involvement in the marketing

effort, the PM is very familiar with the future client's stated and implied needs, budget and operational concerns, method of operation, staffing, etc. Project managers are uniquely prepared to outline a proposed scope of services and to evaluate where adjustments in this scope can occur. In addition, it is vital that the individual who will eventually be responsible for delivering a scope of services to the client be involved in the preparation of that scope.

6. *Develop a detailed project budget.* The project manager must, in the development of the project scope, be aware of the costs required to complete the proposed scope of work. The PM must assemble a detailed project budget and outline areas where the budget can be altered by a change in scope or by negotiations. Without this total understanding of the proposed project budget and scope, the negotiation process will be needlessly complicated. Only a project manager who has actually prepared the project budget can be held accountable for it.

7. *Participate in the negotiation process.* With full understanding of the proposed scope and budget, the project manager is invaluable during final negotiations with the client. Any adjustments that need to be made should be based on the PM's evaluation of the program and the ability of the firm to make an adequate fee and profit for its work. No commitments should be made to the client without the project manager's understanding and approval.

8. *Provide input into future personnel and other resource requirements.* A successful marketing effort commits the firm to supplying personnel and other resources to the client's project. The project manager must fully understand these needs and communicate with other managers to ensure their availability. This is an extension of the marketing effort, in that failure to plan for these needs affects the service provided to the client.

9. *Provide the firm with continued contact with the client.* In all firms, on completion of a project, personnel and resources are turned to other efforts. As a result, many past clients are inadvertently neglected and little follow-up is conducted on project and building performance. When the client is in need of future professional help, much, if not all, contact with the design firm may have been lost. To prevent this, the project manager must contact the client regularly (perhaps two to three times a year). The project manager must also be aware of opportunities to suggest changes or improvements in the existing facility to the client.

In addition, project managers should be alert to opportunities to inform clients of the firm's other services. Often, clients have a perception of your firm based on the services you are currently providing to them. Clients may be unaware of your firm's other capabilities and thus not consider your firm when awarding other projects.

Every staff member has a responsibility to assist in the marketing effort. Project managers, however, are in a unique position to provide job leads, make new contacts, and become involved in community and professional organizations. It is through these efforts that the project manager can also contribute to improving the success of the firm's marketing program.

Survey Findings

The effectiveness of project managers can strongly influence project profitability. Their level of training is an important factor in improving and maintaining effectiveness. Unfortunately, the level of spending by design firms on training is inadequate. Significantly, 27 of the 110 firms (24.5 percent) participating in the APM survey had no documented training expenditures. The mean percentage spent annually on training was 2.59 percent (median 2.0 percent).

Table 4.1 lists the leading responsibilities of project managers as reported by participants in this survey.

A number of significant activities are not considered to be a normal part of a PM's responsibilities by many firms. Table 4.2 lists the responsibilities least mentioned by those participating in the survey.

TABLE 4.1   Project Manager Responsibilities

Responsibility	Number	Percent
Budget preparation	99	90.0
Client meeting/contact	99	90.0
Scope determination	98	89.1
Specifications	95	86.4
Change-order management	92	83.6
Quality assurance/control	88	80.0
Developing a project checklist	87	79.1
Project team meetings	86	78.2
Consultant meetings	84	76.4
On-site observation	82	74.5
Project closeout/evaluation	81	73.6
Proposal preparation	81	73.6
Project status report preparation/review	80	72.7
Personnel planning	70	63.6
Construction administration management	65	59.1

TABLE 4.2   Least-Mentioned PM Responsibilities

Responsibility	Number	Percent
Negotiating owner/designer contracts	38	34.5
Negotiating consultant/designer contracts	40	36.4
Marketing	43	39.1
Project follow-up/postoccupancy evaluation	47	42.7
Program preparation	55	50.0
Selection of consultants	56	50.9
Fee determination	56	50.9
Time-card approval	57	51.8
Billing preparation/review and/or collection	57	51.8
Vendor expense review/approval	60	54.5

5

Caring for Your Project Managers

Finding Project Managers

A continuing source of difficulty for many design firms is finding and recruiting capable project managers. As noted in Chap. 3, since few engineering or architectural schools teach management skills to any degree, it is no wonder that there is a significant shortage of skilled project managers. As increasing numbers of firms recognize the value of project management, the competition for available talent is nearing crisis proportions.

In large cities, high job mobility creates the opportunity to recruit project managers from other firms. In many smaller cities, however, the total architectural and engineering community may number only in the hundreds. As a result, experienced managers may be unavailable or cannot be recruited from other local firms or from larger cities.

For many firms, there are three basic techniques in obtaining the project management talent required:

Recruit from outside your firm

This method is often the fastest approach to building your management staff. However, recruiting from other local firms (particularly in smaller communities) may create animosity on the part of your peers, and it may also eliminate any hesitancy other firms have had about raiding your staff. In addition, the local design community may be somewhat inbred and firms may simply be exchanging each other's weaknesses.

If the local pool of talent is thin, recruiting from other, usually larger, cities, may be the solution. Unfortunately, attracting staff to smaller communities may not be possible when highly paid, experienced project managers are sought. Offering competitive salaries, fringe benefits and ownership (or potential) has been used with varying success.

Train your own project managers

In some communities, the only significant source of project managers may be in a firm's own staff. Some firms are reluctant to make a major investment in training their staff for fear of incurring the expense only to lose these people to competing firms after a few years. Clearly, a certain percentage of your staff will leave the firm for various reasons. With sufficient incentive (salary, bonus, ownership, profit sharing, etc.), many capable staff members will remain to help the firm prosper. These individuals will have made the cost of training well worthwhile.

The training process requires constant budgeting of time and resources for seminars, courses, publications, etc. Some firms recruit prospects directly from colleges and universities to obtain the most capable talent. They then educate these individuals into project managers compatible with their firm's philosophy.

In large cities, successful firms with experienced teams of project managers also seek younger talent and bring them along as assistant project managers to fill needed slots. In many locations, it is not unusual to find a large percentage of design professionals who have worked for one or two local firms at one time. Many of these firms are noted for their training programs.

Recruit an experienced project manager as the mainstay of your staff

For many firms not experienced with effective project management, it is often wise to recruit one knowledgeable manager as the center of your system. This individual should help establish the project management program, recruit and train younger staff, and serve as a technical and managerial resource. In many firms it is not necessary to recruit an experienced manager, since a principal may wish to begin an intensive self-education program to acquire the necessary skills.

Keeping Your Managers

Finding and training your project managers is only the first step. Keeping your hard-won managers is just as important. It is the responsibility of senior management to provide for the psychological and financial well-being of these individuals. The obvious incentives of competitive salaries, bonuses, profit sharing, and a fringe benefit package are most important. As noted in earlier chapters, project managers must have the authority that matches their level of responsibility in the firm. Second-guessing and countermanding their decisions will quickly destroy your project management system. As a result, many of your managers may become interested in opportunities with other firms.

How Many Project Managers Do You Need?

A frequently asked question is "How many project managers does a design firm need?" Unfortunately, there is no fixed answer for a number or reasons.

1. The experience level of your project managers is an important factor. Generally, more experienced PMs should be able to handle more projects. They should also be capable of managing projects of greater complexity than managers with less experience. In many cases, firms employing less experienced managers may require a greater number of individuals to handle the work load.

2. The experience level of your technical staff is a factor. Staff experienced in a particular project type can make the PM's job a great deal easier. Their familiarity with the workings of the firm's project management system is also important. All employees knowing how to best perform their own job can improve efficiency and communications. This allows project managers to focus on important activities.

3. The quality of your support and management information systems will affect the ability of project managers to perform. Effective project management requires a wide array of tools and systems. When managers lack all or part of these systems, more time is required to complete their project responsibilities. This may mean the firm will need a greater number of PMs.

4. The complexity of the specific project a manager handles will affect the manager's ability to manage additional projects. Managing complicated medical or manufacturing facilities will require greater effort and attention than basic speculative office buildings or retail spaces. Increased time demands may be placed on a project manager to administer a complex project.

5. The geographic location of projects will affect the manager's time. Projects located in distant or remote locations will involve more travel time for client meetings, job site visits, and general coordination.

6. Experienced and sophisticated clients can ease the burden on your project managers. The smooth functioning relationship between the project manager and an experienced client can allow a PM to han-

dle additional projects. Occasionally, the sophisticated client can actually require more of a project manager's time by demanding additional services or attention. However, this may be preferred to the "hand-holding" required with an inexperienced client.

7. A major factor determining the number of required project managers is the general staff experience level with the current projects of the firm. When a one-of-a-kind, rarely handled project type is encountered, the learning curve is higher for all. Increased levels of research will be required as will increased levels of client interaction. This will usually necessitate greater time commitments for the PM.

8. The current number of projects under contract is an important factor. Most project managers can handle several projects at one time. An increased number of jobs in the office will result in a higher work load per PM or it will require the hiring or training of additional project managers.

9. The mix of projects normally handled by the firm can affect the number of project managers. For example, an office with a large number of small projects will likely need more PMs than one with a few large jobs. Since most projects need at least a minimum level of service, more jobs means a higher work load.

10. The timing of your projects can put extraordinary demands on project managers. Most firms strive to have PMs handling projects in differing phases to avoid "crunches." Typically, one project may be in a start-up phase, another heavily into design or construction documents. A third may be in construction administration. Unfortunately, delays and changing programs may alter this desired scheme. At those times, the pressure on project managers to perform can be extreme.

With no easy way to determine the required number of project managers, how do firms cope? Well-managed firms always train younger staff in the principles and applications of project management. Junior staff can learn project managment by assisting experienced PMs. After a little seasoning, they are given the opportunity to manage their own smaller, less complicated projects. In this way, a cadre of people is always available to meet the needs of an ever-changing workload.

In small firms with limited staff, all employees should be given basic project management training. It is vital that the required tools and systems are in place to assist in managing projects.

Rewarding Project Managers

Senior managers in many firms find it difficult to determine appropriate rewards for project managers. As key employees of the firm, project managers deserve a high level of base compensation. In most parts of the country, project manager salaries begin at no less than $35,000 and can range upward of $70,000 in major cities and in large firms.

Beyond base salary, what are the best methods to reward project managers? Smart firm managers generally try to assign their best project managers to the most difficult projects. This may be the most technically complicated job, one that has a tight time schedule, or one with a very restrictive fee budget. Basing a project manager's rewards on the project's eventual profit level will be extremely unfair to the good performer assigned to a tough job.

Some firms have attempted to base both the project manager's reward and that of the entire project team on the final profit level of the job. During the fee-budgeting process, senior management and the project manager set a target profit level for the project. It is agreed that any profits beyond that level are divided among the members of the project team, with the manager receiving as much as half.

While this concept appears to be a good idea in theory, in practice it often fails. Human nature indicates that the major effort of the team members will be directed toward the project with the greatest potential for financial reward to the possible detriment of other jobs.

Positive rewards

Provide an atmosphere conducive to positive self-esteem. Project managers must not only have a high level of responsibility, but must also have a corresponding level of authority. Senior management must not only trust the judgment of project managers, but must also publicly back their decisions even if private follow-up is required.

Project managers must also have significant input to decisions for which they will later be held accountable. For example, a project fee budget should be prepared by the project manager and reviewed by senior management, not the reverse. This process rewards and encourages the project manager by providing a positive environment of trust and confidence.

A spot bonus program is an ideal way to reward good performers and should be used by all firms. While the amount of money is not significant, the symbolism is very important. Salary increases and promotions are obvious rewards for good long-term performance. The use of increased fringe benefits can also be a valuable reward. This might include the providing of a company car or similar reward. Firms should also have a profit sharing or similar program in place to reward all staff members for superior year-long performance.

Salaries

The salaries of project managers vary greatly depending on the office location, responsibilities, experience, and many other factors. In many firms, project managers are the second-highest-paid individuals after the principals. Table 5.1 shows the average salaries of nonprincipal project managers as determined by a salary survey conducted by the Association for Project Managers.

The survey also asked respondents to provide data on both the lowest- and highest-paid nonprincipal project managers. For firms with only one or two PMs, the data reported would cover all individuals in this position.

In the lowest-paid category, 21 individuals earned less than $30,000. This may indicate that these people are not full-charge project managers. The mean salary of the lowest paid PM in responding firms was $35,884. The range was from $15,000 to $60,000.

The range of the highest-paid project manager in the responding firms was even more extreme. The lowest-paid in this category was $20,000 and the highest, $75,000. The average salary of the highest-paid PMs was $47,699, and the median firm's understanding of the role of the project manager affects the salary.

TABLE 5.1   Average Salary of Nonprincipal Project Managers

Range	Frequency	Percent
Less than $30 K*	12	12.0
$30.0 K–$39.9 K	36	36.0
$40.0 K–$49.9 K	34	34.0
$50.0 K–$59.9 K	12	12.0
$60.0 K–$69.9 K	6	6.0
	100	100.0
Missing = 10		

*K means thousand.

Developing a Project Manager's Manual   Among the most important training and management tools for project managers is the project management manual. Unfortunately, very few firms prepare this valuable document. Its general purpose is to document most of the responsibilities and tools required in performing the project management role in a design firm.

The manual should be in a loose-leaf format to facilitate its use and to allow for easy revision. Each section should provide a "sunset" date at which it is to be revised. The manual preparation should be managed by a senior executive, while responsibility for research and writing are assigned to several project managers. The sections must be assigned like a project, with specified due dates and content. A professional editor/writer should prepare the final draft.

Typically, the manual is used as a reference document by experienced project managers, as a training tool for new or less experienced managers, and as an orientation tool for new staff members at the middle and senior levels of the firm. Often, firms provide copies of all or part of their manual to their clients in an effort to inform them of the firm's procedures and methods of operation. This can clarify critical issues in the early stage of a project.

Content In general, a project management manual should include the following:

1. *The firm's project management philosophy and approach.* A brief section on the firm's concept of project management and organization.

2. *The role of the project manager in marketing.* This must include an outline of the firm's marketing plan and structure. In addition, the expected interface of the project manager and the marketing staff should be clearly explained.

3. *Project front-end planning and contractual activities.* This section clarifies the project manager's role in preparing the project program and budget and outlines responsibilities and work assignments. In addition, the role of the manager in the writing and negotiating of contracts must be reviewed. Copies of all required forms should be included for illustration purposes.

4. *Management of the project team.* Responsibilities for meetings, communications, personnel issues, and performance appraisals are outlined in detail in this section. Additionally, consultant and client relation activities (including the handling of out-of-scope items) are discussed in this section and copies of all current forms are included. Detailed project checklists and position descriptions for most project roles are also essential.

5. *Quality control.* Although project managers generally do not conduct quality control reviews themselves, they are responsible for ensuring that a time and budget allocation exists for this activity. They must also require that quality assurance reviews are conducted as scheduled.

6. *Control of budgets and schedules.* Requirements for review of budgets and project status reports must be outlined and standard forms should be included. Standard operating procedures for the administration of these items (particularly change orders) are outlined here. A procedure for corrective actions in the event of problems should be included.

7. *Project closeout and follow-up activities.* Checklists and procedures for completing a project are reviewed in this section. As in other sections of the manual, this section should include samples of all required forms. Instructions for project follow-up and continued contact must be outlined.

Although enhancements to the manual can be included, these sections provide the basic information required. The key to a successful project management manual lies in its completeness and easy use. Any system or manual that becomes too complex or cumbersome will not be used.

Sample Project Management Manual The American Institute of Architects (AIA) has published *Managing Architectural Projects: The Project Management Manual,* by David Haviland. This 112-page book provides guidance in the development of an in-house manual. A prototypical manual is included. (See Fig. 5.1 and Resources for more information.)

I. PROJECT MANAGEMENT APPROACH

A. Statement of firm's overall goals and objectives
B. Statement of project management objectives
C. Overall firm organization
D. Project management organization
E. Position descriptions for each project management role

II. PROJECT CHECKLIST

A detailed statement of project management tasks during each phase of professional services. This may be expanded into a complete project checklist. It may allow modification for individual projects.

III. PROJECT MANAGEMENT POLICIES AND PROCEDURES

A. PLANNING
1. Evaluation of potential projects and clients
2. Interviews and preparation of proposals
3. Proposal format standards
4. Project work plan format standards
5. Delineation of owner and firm requirements and standards
6. Scheduling and budgeting
7. Approval and communication of workplans
8. Maintenance and updating of work plans

B. STAFFING AND ORGANIZATION
1. Negotiation of owner agreements
2. Consultant selection
3. Negotiation of consultant agreements
4. Assignment of in-house staff to projects
5. Project team
6. Initial team briefings: participants, agenda

C. CLIENT RELATIONS
1. Owner contacts
2. Owner correspondence: requirements, formats, logging, etc.
3. Submittals and presentations: attendees, agendas, records, follow-up

D. TEAM RELATIONS
1. Team meetings: frequency, attendees, agendas, minutes
2. Team correspondence: format, distribution

III. PROJECT MANAGEMENT POLICIES AND PROCEDURES (continued)

E. INFORMATION AND DOCUMENTATION
1. Filing system
2. Procedures for technical information, product samples, shop drawings, tests, etc.
3. Project logs and records

F. QUALITY CONTROL
1. Quality assurance process and procedure
2. Checking procedures and forms
3. Standards for project reports
4. Standards for drawings, specifications and other contract documents

G. SCHEDULE, BUDGET AND BILLINGS CONTROL
1. Project authorization: procedure and forms
2. Time authorization, reporting and recording
3. Employee expenses authorization, reporting and recording
4. Consultant expenses authorization, reporting and recording
5. Vendor expenses authorization, reporting and recording
6. Other expenses authorization, reporting and recording
7. Project status reports: frequency, format, distribution, follow-up
8. Projections (status against work plan, effort-to-complete against targets): frequency, responsibility, distribution, follow-up
9. Reports to top management
10. Procedures for authorizing changes in work plan
11. Policy and procedures for client billings and follow-up

H. PROJECT CLOSEOUT AND EVALUATION
1. Project records: permanent files, retention
2. Project evaluation policy and procedure: responsibility, participants, results
3. Project follow-up policy

Figure 5.1 Example outline for the project manager's manual. (*From Managing Architectural Projects: The Process, © 1984 The American Institute of Architects. Reproduced under license number 91105. Further reproduction prohibited.*)

6

Training Project Managers

Few members of your staff are of greater importance to your firm's success than are your project managers. Their pivotal role among clients, contractors, and staff requires them to possess a unique set of skills. Unfortunately, many project managers are forced to learn on the job. The benefits to them and the firm of a formal training program are great. What should a project manager training program include?

Required Skills

There are three broad areas that should be covered: communication skills, interpersonal skills, and technical management skills.

Communication skills

Project managers need to possess a wide range of communication skills. Their importance to the marketing effort is well-documented. Well-managed firms seek to involve these individuals at a very early stage in contacting a potential client. As a result, their experience and skill at marketing and selling is essential. Some firms encourage and pay for project managers to take courses in these topics at local colleges.

Other communications skills are also important to project managers. In particular, negotiating, effective writing, and public speaking are vital to PMs. Their involvement in negotiating contracts and communicating with other members of the project team such as consultants makes this an obvious area of focus for your training efforts. There are a number of commercially available negotiating courses available, such as those offered by Karass Associates and Robert J. Laser Associates.

Many design professionals are poor writers. Much of their writing suffers from wordiness, improper punctuation and capitalization, run-on sentences, and a long list of other grammatical faults. This inability to write effectively and properly reflects poorly on your firm. Many local community colleges and universities such as the University of Wisconsin Department of Engineering Professional Development periodically offer effective writing courses.

There are many speaking opportunities for project managers. Examples include community groups, social organizations, client meetings, project team meetings, and marketing situations. Public speaking is high on most individuals' lists of major fears. This fear is often overcome only through practice. While some project managers practice presentations before the project team or family members, others seek more directed and instructive environments offered by groups such as Toastmasters. This organization has local affiliates in nearly every major U.S. city.

Interpersonal skills

Project managers are people managers. They must know how to direct, motivate, and manage their project team, contractors, clients, suppliers, and many other individuals with whom they interact. For some this is a natural ability; for others it requires extensive training in human psychology. There are numerous sources to help your project managers improve their ability to work with people.

A skill that is very difficult to teach is leadership. Some individuals exhibit natural leadership skills; others can learn techniques to improve their leadership ability.

Perhaps the most difficult skill to learn is that of delegation. Many design professionals tend to be poor delegators; ego-driven, they often lack trust in their subordinates' skills. As a result, these individuals feel the need to be involved in all aspects of the project at all times. Not only does this overburden them, it hinders the performance of project team members. Learning how to delegate is a painstaking process that must be reinforced by the example of top management and by providing the tools and systems to permit adequate supervision of subordinates.

Technical management skills

To be effective, a project manager must have a complete understanding of technical management skills. This covers a broad range of project activities. Project budgeting, scope determination, personnel planning, and quality assurance reviews are only a few of these tasks.

There are a number of outside sources of assistance in developing or enhancing these capabilities. In particular, the American Institute of Architects offers a self-assessment program in project administration [telephone (202) 626-7348]. There are also the annual (held in early January) week-long course offered by the University of Wisconsin Department of Engineering Professional Development and programs offered by a number of local affiliates of the national professional societies. In addition, a number of excellent texts are available on these topics. (See Resources for more information.)

Developing Your Training Program

Most design firms managers are oblivious to the how and why of an ongoing training program. This continuing education of staff and management requires a commitment, a plan, and a budget. Unfortunately, most firms leave this process up to each individual, clearly subjecting the firm's future to chance.

Farsighted design firm managers offer opportunities for staff and management to learn or improve their skills. Methods vary, ranging from in-house seminars to paid tuition at local colleges. Training not only improves skills, but serves as a morale booster and a fringe benefit while protecting the firm's future.

Employee turnover is often the rationalization for not providing formal training. "Why train someone else's staff at our expense?" is the philosophy.

Many high-technology companies experience a significant increase in employee productivity after having developed and funded comprehensive formal training programs. Experience indicates similar results for architects and engineers. It is clear that the cost of training is more than matched by productivity increases and is favorable toward training.

In general, training goals fall into three categories:

1. Teaching employees and managers how to perform a new or unfamiliar task within their current job.
2. Helping employees and managers improve their performance on their present job.
3. Preparing employees and managers to handle new jobs.

Staff/management training

There are two major areas of training for an organization: staff and managerial. Staff training usually consists of enhancing specific skills such as drafting, CADD, and product/service knowledge. Training in these areas is usually very direct, observable, and objective and can be broken into a number of discrete parts or elements.

Managerial training, however, usually focuses on communication skills, supervisory skills, human relations, etc. Although these types of skills are more subjective and harder to quantify and measure, they may have a greater impact on your organization. A firm may have the finest, most talented engineers or architects in the country, but without proper supervision, direction, and motivation, this talent may be unproductive.

Determining if training is needed

Often training is conducted for fairly limited reasons. These include teaching new skills to recent or current employees, retraining employees in skill areas they may have lost or not used in many years, and keeping employees abreast of changes in technology and design.

Your first step in the training process is to determine the need for training. A thorough needs analysis should be performed on the organization by employee and position. In assessing the organization's needs, it is necessary to look at the firm as a whole. What are its strengths and weaknesses, and how does it compare to its competition?

In determining the firm's overall needs, it is necessary to look at both short- and long-term needs. For example, if a senior partner who has handled most of the firm's marketing will be retiring in two years, now is the time to start training a replacement.

It is important at this level of assessment to consider the short- and long-term goals of the firm. These will have an impact on what the training needs are, or will be.

Another important aspect of this organizational assessment is the climate of the firm. The firm's attitude and motivational level will have a great impact on the success of any training programs that are instituted. One method of assessing the general training needs and attitude of staff is to conduct interviews and questionnaire surveys of senior management, project managers, etc.

The second level of assessment, along position lines, will help determine more specifically what training is needed and where. A thorough analysis must be done on each position in the firm to determine not only the duties and responsibilities of the position, but also the needed skills a person must have to successfully do the job.

This type of assessment involves a formal, systematic study of a position that covers a number of items. This includes what persons in each position do in relation to information or other people; what procedures and techniques they use; the equipment, tools, machinery, etc. they need; the products or services that result from their effort; and the skills, traits, and attributes required of the person in the position.

Last, an analysis needs to be done on all employees and partners to determine what skills each person has or lacks. This will help determine what training they may need to better perform their job, what position they can move into next, and what job they could grow into in the future. Assessment of employee skills may involve reviewing performance evaluations, reviewing work, completing questionnaires, and conducting skills or ability tests.

When looked at as a whole, the identification of training needs is an involved and complex procedure. It will, however, allow a firm to assess its strengths and weaknesses, focus attention where needed, and grow in the direction desired.

Few design firms have a well-established training program. Most firms simply take advantage of isolated seminars and, often, only senior management attends these programs. Training is often considered the responsibility of the individual, who is expected to plan, schedule, and finance a program. As a result, most firms are not adequately prepared to respond to the need for new services or to meet changing market conditions.

A staff training program requires a long-term commitment and a recognition that the payback may not be immediate. Regular training will result in a more productive and profitable firm. How should a training program be developed?

1. Have senior management make a commitment to a continuing program. A program that is conducted on an irregular basis will never achieve its goals.

2. Establish an educational planning group composed of three or four individuals representing all staff levels and chaired by a principal. This group should be charged with developing and managing the training program, researching training options and techniques, and preparing specific programs. They should meet regularly (at least once a month) and should operate on a priority basis.

3. Develop a training plan and schedule. This should include choosing various types of training programs, establishing training priorities and goals, and outlining who is eligible for each program. In addition, a schedule should be established to control the training process.

4. Establish a training budget as part of the annual budgeting process conducted by the firm. These are funds that should be spent and not viewed as an area to cut if the firm experiences temporary declines in workload.

5. Inform your staff of the various training options available and what items the firm will pay for.

6. Require those attending outside educational programs to disseminate their information to other staff members. This could be done at lunch meetings where short presentations are made, or in a summary report on the program.

7. Vary the types of training programs used. Many options are available, including:

- *In-house lectures and seminars.* These programs may last from 1 hour to 1 day, and they may be conducted by outside management consultants and specialty consultants, building product manufacturers, college professors, or experienced, knowledgeable staff members.
- *College courses.* Tuition may be paid in part or in full for certain staff members to expand present capabilities or develop new ones. Correspondence courses should also be considered.
- *Outside seminars.* The National Society of Professional Engineers (NSPE), American Consulting Engineers Council (ACEC), and many other organizations sponsor numerous part-day, full-day, and multiday courses and seminars in major cities. Many universities (particularly the University of Wisconsin, Pennsylvania State University, and Harvard University) regularly offer short seminar courses. Although the cost of attending many of these programs is high, they give staff and principals the opportunity to exchange information and ideas with individuals from firms throughout the country.
- *Professional conferences and conventions.* These may include conventions and conferences organized by professional design groups (AIA, ACEC, NSPE, etc.), suppliers, product manufacturers, client groups (American Hospital Association, etc.), and others.
- *Audio and video tapes.* Although many of these tapes are too short, poorly produced, and expensive, some may have lasting value as reference and refresher tools.
- *Resource materials.* An important part of a good training program is a library of reference books, magazines, etc. This material must be organized into a usable collection that is regularly maintained and updated.

8. Review the performance of your training program. At least once a year, the entire program should be reviewed for its effectiveness, cost, and impact on morale and productivity. The budget must be evaluated for its short- and long-term cost-effectiveness.

What makes for effective learning?

Probably the most critical factor determining the success of training is the motivation and attitude of the people being trained. The trainees should want to be trained and should believe that the training will have positive results. There are a number of steps that can be taken to help foster these feelings, before and during the training process. The most important is that the goals and desired outcomes be conveyed to the trainees.

During training sessions, there should be rewards for learning the material. Reinforcement must be provided for making use of what was learned and for proper learning or training behavior. Trainees will learn and remember material that they consider to be meaningful and important.

Every training program should begin with an overview of the material to be covered and an explanation of how it relates back to job problems or performance. The material should be broken into logical pieces, and these should be put into a rational, progressive sequence. The terms used and the technology discussed should be familiar to the trainees. New terms and technology should be presented in a manner that the trainees can relate to. Visual aids should be used whenever possible.

Training Practice and Methods

There are a number of different methods by which training materials can be presented. The method of presentation will determine the effectiveness of the program. No single method can be used for all types of material. A training program should be designed for maximum efficiency within the constraints of time, cost, location, equipment availability, etc.

Lecture method

Probably the most familiar and widely used instructional method is the lecture. It is usually done live, but it may be presented on videotape or audio tape. From a training and learning standpoint, the lecture is one of the weakest methods. It usually involves no interaction, practice, study, or testing of the material presented.

Classroom training

Traditional classroom training is basically a series of lectures. Classroom training allows for modifications and enhancements to the lecture method by providing workbooks, small group discussions and practice, multiple sessions with homework, regular testing, etc. This approach is certainly more effective than a simple lecture and is appropriate for more complicated training. In a design firm, it could be adopted for almost any type of staff training. This could include specific technical skills, such as drafting, drawing, CADD, etc. This is especially true when enhanced with a lab setup, using CADD terminals or drafting, for hands-on practice.

Programmed learning

Probably the best method, at least for skills training, is programmed learning. This method breaks the training program down into many smaller parts that are put into a logical sequence. At the end of each section or module, the participants are tested and given immediate feedback as to their understanding of the material. Training courses of this type are much more difficult and costly to develop, and they usually involve programmed texts or workbooks. There are many advantages to this type of training approach. It is designed to be individually paced, with each participant moving at an individual speed. Frequent testing can determine whether the material is being learned.

Group discussion

This method is very familiar to most professionals and can be used as a separate approach in and of itself, or in conjunction with lectures. In this method, small groups discuss issues or problems and work out new ideas, solutions, proposals, etc. It is most effective for teaching problem-solving and decision-making skills, presenting complicated or difficult material, or changing opinions and attitudes. As such, it is probably most useful for management, rather than staff-level, training. It is particularly useful in human relations, communications, and supervisor training programs. Depending on the nature of the material covered, it may include intense confrontation and discussion or argument, role playing, case studies, management games, simulation exercises, etc.

This section is only an overview of training program approaches. All of these programs can be used either in-house or at outside locations, but are typically conducted off the job, or off-site. These approaches take the trainees away from their regular jobs. In many cases, programs away from the work site will result in a more productive learning atmosphere.

On-the-job training

Another type of training method is on-the-job training (OJT). This is often used in training for specific skills. Trainees learn while they are actually on the job and are being productive. OJT is usually combined with classroom training or other off-the-job approaches as well. Internships are an example of this approach. In a design firm, the OJT approach may be used for drafting, CADD, design work, etc. Firms often combine the OJT method with other approaches for better results.

Program evaluation

The purpose of a training program is to increase employee and organizational performance and productivity. The evaluation of any training should therefore focus on measuring these factors.

Managing the Training Program

A decision must be made whether to develop and provide training in-house or to purchase programs from outside vendors. There are advantages and disadvantages to either approach. A primary consideration in deciding to start in-house is whether you have the expertise and the facilities to do so.

Another major consideration is your budget. There is a cost to providing training. As with any other project, costs need to be determined and a budget established. The overall budget must cover a number of items. These include training materials and supplies, facility use/rental, instructors' salaries, price/cost per trainee, plus the loss of productivity while the trainees are off the job. As a rule, a design firm should spend at least 5 percent of its annual total revenues on training.

Consideration must be given to a program's timing as well, to determine what month, week, or days of the week are most convenient. The location and facility must be chosen. Participants, supervisors, and managers must be notified of all details.

Some of the above steps can be eliminated if a decision is made to go with an outside training provider. However, careful effort should be put into evaluation and choosing an outside provider.

Sources/providers

There are literally thousands of outside providers of training programs. Most, if not all, professional organizations, such as the AIA, either conduct or sponsor professional training. The American Society for Training and Development (ASTD) is an organization that would be a valuable contact. The same is true for the American Society for Personnel Administration (ASPA). (See Resources for more information on these organizations.) Other providers of training services are management consulting firms, industrial psychologists, and colleges, universities, and other schools.

Numerous books have also been published on the subject of training. Check with local and university libraries for titles on this subject.

Training of young staff should begin immediately on graduation.

The AIA has developed an excellent method called the Intern Development Program (IDP). This program provides a structured framework that exposes young, unlicensed architects to the specific areas of practice required to pass state licensing exams and eventually contribute to their employers' practices. The IDP also provides special advisors and offers a series of study guides covering all areas of architectural practice.

As noted earlier in this chapter, the AIA has developed a self-assessment program. Under this program, a practitioner can complete an examination on a subject and receive a grade to determine which areas require further attention.

Planning
the Project

7

The Firm's Profit Plan

In a national survey of design firms conducted by Birnberg & Associates, one question addressed the issue of the preparation of annual profit plans. Out of 152 firms responding, 108, or 71 percent, prepared such plans. Many of these firms were large, successful companies. Unfortunately, many small firms fail to follow suit.

A profit plan is defined as a *management tool for formalizing the firm's financial objectives.*

The benefits of preparing a plan are many, including:

1. Establishing yearly goals

2. Providing intermediate targets throughout the year

The remainder of this chapter will discuss how to prepare a profit plan and apply it.

Table 7.1 provides a blank form which you may copy for your immediate use. Tables 7.2 to 7.5 isolate portions of the plan for discussion. Note that consultant and nonconsultant reimbursables and the markup on reimbursables are not considered on the profit plan. The profit plan is prepared in the same manner whether you manage your firm on a cash or accrual basis (not on your tax basis).

Labor

Table 7.2 isolates the portion of the profit plan concerned with labor allocation. Labor for the firm has two components, project-chargeable (direct expense) and non-project-chargeable (overhead). Each principal's time is analyzed on the basis of historical records and future projections of work load for the breakdown of project-chargeable versus

TABLE 7.1 Profit Plan

	Total	Project expenses	Overhead	Profit
Principals' draw	$ _____	$	$	$
__ % project-assigned		_____		
__ % unassigned			_____	
Technical salaries	_____			
__ % project-assigned		_____		
__ % unassigned			_____	
Administrative salaries	_____			
__ % project-assigned		_____		
__ % unassigned			_____	
1. Total labor	_____	_____	_____	
2. Nonreimbursables	_____	_____	_____	
3. Overhead	_____	_____	_____	
4. Net profit (before tax)	_____			_____
5. Net fees	_____	_____	_____	_____

			Target	
Income statement		Percent	Time-card ratio	
Net fees	$ _____	_____		
Labor	- _____	_____	1.0	
Nonreimbursables	- _____	_____	_____	
Gross profit	_____	_____	_____	
Overhead	- _____	_____	_____	
Net profit (before tax)	_____	_____	_____	

SOURCE: Adapted from *Profit: Planning for It, Making It and Keeping It*, by Douglas A. Bevis, AIA, Naramore, Bain, Brady and Johanson, Seattle, 1976.

TABLE 7.2 Sample Profit Plan—Labor Only

	Total	Project expenses	Overhead
Principals' draw	$150,000	$	$
60% project-assigned		90,000	
40% unassigned			60,000
Technical salaries	350,000		
83% project-assigned		290,000	
17% unassigned			60,000
Administrative salaries	100,000		
20% project-assigned		20,000	
80% unassigned			80,000
1. Total labor	$600,000	$400,000	$200,000

NOTE: All figures are for illustrative purposes only and should not be used as targets for your firm.

non-project-chargeable. An overall average for all principals is calculated and entered as in Table 7.2 (60 percent project-assigned and 40 percent unassigned). The importance of complete and accurate time sheets is readily seen.

A total figure for the principals' draw is prepared (exclusive of bonuses, profit sharing, etc.). As shown in Table 7.2, this amount is $150,000 for the year. Hence

$150,000 × 60% = $90,000 direct expense (project assigned)

$150,000 × 40% = $60,000 overhead (unassigned)

This same process is repeated for the technical staff and administrative staff. The 20 percent project-assigned value for the administrative staff often comes from secretaries typing specifications, reports, etc. Each heading (total, project expenses, overhead) is totaled to achieve the total labor line. Required to complete this section are:

1. Total salaries and a breakdown by principals (or partners), technical staff, and administrative staff projected for the coming year

2. Estimated chargeable rates for each principal and staff member projected for the coming year

Nonlabor Costs

Table 7.3 adds all other costs (other than labor) to the plan. Nonreimbursable direct expenses are project-chargeable expenses that come out of your fee. This would include such items as printing, entertainment, travel, some consultants, and other similar expenses.

TABLE 7.3 Sample Profit Plan and Nonlabor Costs

	Total	Project expenses	Overhead	Profit
Principals' draw	$ 150,000	$	$	$
60% project-assigned		90,000		
40% unassigned			60,000	
Technical salaries	350,000			
83% project-assigned		290,000		
17% unassigned			60,000	
Administrative salaries	100,000			
20% project-assigned		20,000		
80% unassigned			80,000	
1. Total labor	$ 600,000	$400,000	$200,000	
2. Nonreimbursables	10,000	10,000		
3. Overhead	400,000		400,000	
4. Net profit (before tax)	390,000			390,000
5. Net fees (revenues)	$1,400,000	$410,000	$600,000	$390,000

Since these expenses are all project-related, they are listed under direct expenses. In general, you should seek to minimize these expenses.

Overhead totals are established by performing a detailed analysis of projected expenses (including all fringe benefits) for the coming year. In Table 7.3, it is estimated that overhead expenses for the coming year will be $400,000, as listed under the *Overhead* column.

Net profit (before tax) is determined by the establishment of attainable profit goals by the firm's principals. For partnerships, this figure would be the total of the partners' desired shares in addition to salary draw and any planned distribution to the staff. A reasonable profit target is 17 to 20 percent of total revenues (without reimbursables) or 25 percent of net revenues. The example shown in Table 7.3 indicates a target net profit of 27.9 percent:

$$\frac{390,000}{1,400,000} = 27.9\%$$

According to the profit plan, the firm has targeted $1.4 million in net revenues for the year. Net revenues are those earned by your efforts only and do not include any pass-through items such as general reimbursables, consultant reimbursables, and consultant nonreimbursable direct expenses. In the event that the economy or other factors will not permit this level of revenues, a rebudgeting should be performed. Remember, this is a work sheet and should be recalculated on the basis of new information and/or conditions.

Ratios and Multipliers

Net revenues (total or gross revenue less general reimbursables and all consultants) are the basis for calculation at 100 percent, and each line item is converted to a percentage of revenues.

$$\frac{400,000 \text{ (direct labor)}}{1,400,000 \text{ (net revenues)}} = 28.6\%$$

Each item is calculated in the same manner.

A time-card ratio or multiplier is calculated by using direct labor (i.e., total raw labor without fringes) as a base of 1. All other items are expressed as a factor of direct labor. For example: net revenues/direct labor is

$$\frac{1,400,000}{400,000} = 3.5$$

$$\frac{\text{Total overhead}}{\text{direct labor}} = \frac{600,000}{400,000} = 1.5$$

$$\frac{\text{Nonreimbursables}}{\text{direct labor}} = \frac{10,000}{400,000} = 0.25$$

$$\frac{\text{Net profit}}{\text{direct labor}} = \frac{390,000}{400,000} = 0.975$$

If a firm's 3.5 multiplier (based on direct raw labor without fringes) is too high for the local market conditions, then overhead or other factors can be adjusted to reduce the multiplier. (Once the multiplier is changed, recalculate the profit plan to review its impact on profit.) A gross multiplier would include a factor for most consultants and reimbursable expenses.

A profit plan will provide:

1. Revenue and profit goals to aim for and measure progress against

2. Information for pricing new work including a multiplier, overhead rate, and billing rates

3. Chargeable rates in total and by employee

4. Salary budget in total which provides a target amount for raises for the year

5. Overhead and marketing budgets

6. Marketing goals (total volume of work required to achieve goals)

Keep in mind that, at year's end, it is unlikely that all the targets indicated on your profit plan will be achieved, but as experience grows, plans will become increasingly more accurate.

Determining a Multiplier

Table 7.4 produces an income statement based on line 5 of the profit plan. This income statement is used to produce percentage targets and a firm multiplier, as shown in Table 7.5.

Financial Ratios for Project Managers

There are many financial ratios that can be calculated, but several stand out as most important for project managers.

Net profit ratios

This bottom-line analysis of profitability has four variations. One variation may be more meaningful to you than another, depending on your method of doing business.

TABLE 7.4   Sample Profit Plan and Income Statement

	Total	Project expenses	Overhead	Profit
Principals' draw	$ 150,000	$	$	$
60% project-assigned		90,000		
40% unassigned			60,000	
Technical salaries	350,000			
83% project-assigned		290,000		
17% unassigned			60,000	
Administrative salaries	100,000			
20% project-assigned		20,000		
80% unassigned			80,000	
1. Total labor	$ 600,000	$400,000	$200,000	
2. Nonreimbursables	10,000	10,000		
3. Overhead	400,000		400,000	
4. Net profit (before tax)	390,000			390,000
5. Net fees (revenues)	$ 1,400,000	$410,000	$600,000	$390,000

Income Statement	
Net fees	$ 1,400,000
Labor	– 400,000
Nonreimbursables	– 10,000
Gross profit	$ 990,000
Overhead	– 600,000
Net profit (before tax)	$ 390,000

TABLE 7.5   Income Statement and Percentage Targets

Income statement		Target	
		Percent	Time-card ratio
Net fees	$ 1,400,000	100.0	3.500
Labor	– 400,000	28.6	1.000
Nonreimbursables	– 10,000	0.7	0.025
Gross profit	$ 990,000	70.7	2.475
Overhead	– 600,000	42.9	1.500
Net profit (before tax)	$ 390,000	27.9	0.975

1. *Net profit on net revenues (before distributions).*   Net revenues are those earned by the firm after pass-through items such as nonreimbursable consultants and other reimbursables are deducted. In this ratio, profitability is measured before distributions of profit, bonus, and any other discretionary distributions.

$$\frac{\text{Net profit}}{\text{net revenues}} = \text{profit percentage}$$

This ratio is particularly meaningful for firms that do not regularly pay year-end bonuses or profit sharing and wish to analyze profit only on their own revenues.

2. *Net profit on net revenues (after distributions).* This ratio is calculated in the same manner as the before-distributions ratio except that bonus, profit sharing, and other discretionary distributions of profit are deducted before the calculation is made. Most firms charge these distributions to overhead. If you pay these various distributions each year and consider them a cost of doing business, then this calculation would be useful.

3. *Net profit on total revenues (before distributions).* For firms that use few outside consultants and have a minimal level of reimbursable expenses, profit measured on total (gross) revenues is more useful.

$$\frac{\text{Net profit}}{\text{total revenues}} = \text{profit percentage}$$

4. *Net profit on total revenues (after distributions).* This ratio is calculated in the same manner as ratio 3 above, except that an after-distribution base is used.

Overhead ratios

Overhead evaluation and reduction is one of the most significant concerns for project and firm managers. This important ratio can be calculated two ways:

1. *Overhead rate (before distributions).* As noted earlier, discretionary distributions are customarily charged to overhead. As a result, a before-distributions calculation of overhead will provide an accurate ratio for those firms that do not consider discretionary distributions to be a cost of doing business. The overhead rate is calculated as follows:

$$\frac{\text{Total firm overhead}}{\text{total firm direct labor}} = \text{overhead rate}$$

Direct labor is based only on raw labor without fringes (which are charged to overhead).

2. *Overhead rate (after distributions).* This ratio is calculated the same as in no. 1 except that total firm overhead now includes discretionary distributions of profit.

Net multiplier

The net multiplier is calculated by dividing net revenues by total firm direct labor:

$$\frac{\text{Net revenues}}{\text{total firm direct labor}} = \text{net multiplier}$$

This ratio indicates the effective markup a firm is achieving for each $1 of direct labor expense (not direct personnel expense, which includes fringe benefits). It is not your target multiplier, but your actual multiplier achieved.

Chargeable rate

The chargeable rate is significant because it measures total (or technical staff) time actually charged to projects (whether billed or not). It measures staff utilization and should be maximized. It is calculated as follows:

$$\frac{\text{Total firm direct labor}}{\text{direct labor} + \text{fringes} + \text{indirect labor}} = \text{chargeable rate}$$

All values in the denominator are based on totals for the firm.

Productivity Measures

There are two major productivity measures every firm should calculate, but recognize that these are imperfect, as noted below.

1. *Net revenues per total staff.* This productivity measure determines how many fee dollars you derive from each staff member:

$$\frac{\text{Net revenue}}{\text{total staff}} = \text{net revenues per total staff}$$

Total staff includes all technical staff, principals, support staff, and all part-timers (adjusted as full-time equivalents).

2. *Net revenues per total staff.* This productivity measure is calculated the same as no. 1 above, except only technical staff and principals are included in the calculation.

It is actually very difficult to determine the productivity level of design office staff. For years, many CADD vendors and software manufacturers have been promoting the productivity gains achieved by using their equipment and programs. Often, these claims have been based on vague measures. Typically, the time required to produce a detail or sheet of drawings is the yardstick. Unfortunately, these manufacturers fail to measure the time and effort required to achieve the capability to complete the drawing on CADD. They also do not directly relate the economic value of that accomplishment to the firm.

Many design firms try to relate productivity to economic value. As discussed above, the most common method of achieving this relationship is to use net revenues per total staff. This factor relates the net (without consultants and reimbursables) dollar amount of revenues billed (not necessarily collected) per each total staff member.

While this factor ties productivity to economic value, it contains some inherent weaknesses. For example, if the marketing staff within a firm is unable to maintain a steady flow of new work, then it is of little consequence that the technical staff is highly efficient. An additional problem results if project managers or principals are poor negotiators or do not carefully manage the scope of services; their projects may reach maximums more quickly then if project administration were more effective.

A highly productive staff may not translate into profits if project fees are set at an insufficient level to cover the cost structure of the firm. Despite the difficulties in using the revenues per employee calculation, it can still be of great value to firm managers. And it is superior to measures of productivity based simply on time calculations.

Average Collection Period

This financial measure calculates the length of time required from the date of billing to the date of collection. This measure is directly reflected in cash-flow measures. The two-step calculation is

Step 1:
$$\frac{\text{Annual total revenues}}{365 \ (\text{days in the year})} = \text{average day's sales}$$

Step 2:
$$\frac{\text{Average accounts receivable}}{\text{average days sales}} = \text{days}$$

Scope Determination

There are many methods that design firms use to determine the scope of services on a project. Many work with detailed checklists. Some use approximate guidelines and others simply use the broad definition of services offered in the AIA's and other organizations' standard-form contracts.

Analysis of Activities

A preferred method requires detailed analysis of the activities needed to complete the project. This list of activities can be reviewed with the client and a determination made as to those for which the designer is responsible. An excellent planning tool for determining your scope of services is the AIA's Compensation Guidelines System (see Resources for specific publications). This system provides a series of phase-by-phase formats listing detailed activities. Although architectural descriptions are shown, minor changes could easily make the formats useful for engineers or interior designers. Figure 8.1 shows a sample worksheet that can be used for determining the project scope.

Typically, the architect uses this series of forms to inform the client of the variety of available services. Additional services, such as graphic design, could be added if requested by the client or suggested by the designer. Disagreements over who is to provide a service or is responsible for an activity can be minimized by notation under the appropriate heading across the top. Separate compensation methods could be indicated as shown, although this should be kept reasonably consistent to avoid confusion.

Although this is an excellent tool for determining a scope of services, this system has significant drawbacks as a management and monitoring tool. Its complexity makes filling out time sheets in such

SCHEDULE OF DESIGNATED SERVICES WORKSHEET	By Architect	By Architect, as Outside Services		By Owner, Coordinated by Architect	By Owner			By Architect, as Additional Service*	Not to be Provided	Method of Compensation
PHASE 5: CONSTRUCTION DOCUMENTS SERVICES										
Project_____ Project #_____ Date_____ Owner_____ Architect_____										
5.01 Project Administration										
5.02 Disciplines Coordination/Document Checking										
5.03 Agency Consulting/Review/Approval										
5.04 Owner-supplied Data Coordination										
5.21 Architectural Design/Documentation										
5.22 Structural Design/Documentation										
5.23 Mechanical Design/Documentation										
5.24 Electrical Design/Documentation										
5.25 Civil Design/Documentation										
5.26 Landscape Design/Documentation										
5.27 Interior Design/Documentation										
5.28 Materials Research/Specifications										
5.30 Special Bidding Documents/Scheduling										
5.32 Statement of Probable Construction Cost										
5.33 Presentations										

Reproduced with permission of The American Institute of Architects under license number 91105. Permission expires August 1, 1992. FURTHER REPRODUCTION IS PROHIBITED.

Because AIA Documents are revised from time to time, users should ascertain from the AIA the current edition of this document. Copies of the current edition of this AIA document may be purchased from The American Institute of Architects or its local distributors.

The text of this document is not "model language" and is not intended for use in other documents without permission of the AIA.

METHODS OF COMPENSATION

A = Multiple of Direct Salary Expense
B = Multiple of Direct Personnel Expense
C = Professional Fee Plus Expenses
D = Percentage of Construction Cost

E = Stipulated Sum
F = Hourly Billing Rates
G = Multiple of Amounts Billed to Architect
H = Other:

*Requires separate authorization and compensation

AIA® FORM F815 · DESIGNATED SERVICES WORKSHEET, PHASE 5 · JANUARY 1978 EDITION · © 1978   THE AMERICAN INSTITUTE OF ARCHITECT:
THE AMERICAN INSTITUTE OF ARCHITECTS, 1735 NEW YORK AVE., N.W., WASHINGTON, DC 20006   FINANCIAL MANAGEMENT SYSTEM

Figure 8.1 Sample completed schedule of designated services work sheet (form F818). (*From Managing Architectural Projects: The Process, © 1984 The American Institute of Architects.*)

detail nearly impossible. Project status reports showing this extensive detail would be impossibly complex.

Dividing Contracts

Many design firms are dividing their contracts into three or more separate parts. For example, scope determination, programming, and possibly preliminary design work is handled as one contract often billed to the client on a time-card basis. A second contract is then prepared once the detailed requirements of the project have been determined. A third contract is prepared for the construction administration phase. Some clients even hire outside specialty firms for this last activity.

Selecting Outside Consultants

The early selection of outside consultants to join the project team is an extremely important decision. This allows their input into the scope definition process and ensures that all parties are in agreement on responsibilities and financial issues. Many designers work with consultants with whom they have a long-standing relationship. Unfortunately, these individuals or firms may not have the best technical qualifications or be best suited to meet the clients' needs.

The lead design firm must be very thorough and careful in the selection of outside consultants to join the project team. Failure to exercise proper care could result in delays, lower profits, and even lawsuits.

The selection process

Every design firm that recommends consultants to clients should have a well-established process to evaluate these firms. Otherwise, you may be doing a disservice to your client and to yourself. This evaluation process should include the following steps:

1. Establish a resource file of capable consultants. This should include information on their specialty, if any, as well as any other pertinent data. This material should be updated regularly by your marketing staff or principals. This file is much like that maintained by many of your clients on you and your peers.
2. Develop an evaluation system for consultants who have worked on your past projects. This will provide ready reference material on their performance, staffs, methods of operation, etc.
3. Maintain materials and an evaluation on consultants with whom you are very familiar. You may, however, include them on your

short list without an extended evaluation. Always consider other consultants. You may find them better able to meet your (and your clients') needs.

4. Collect information on consultants with whom you have not worked. This includes:
   a. A list of references of several other prime design firms with whom they have worked.
   b. Biographical data on individuals who will be assigned to your project. Obviously, this must include information that convinces you of their managerial or technical capability.
   c. Information on the consultant's financial ability. If possible, obtain a financial statement. Your primary concerns are that the consultant can afford to add staff if necessary and to provide the required project personnel. It is also important that the consultant can afford additional office space if needed, can meet the higher professional liability premiums that the additional work may require, etc.
   d. Data on the consultant's internal management structure and project delivery methods. It is a great help if their method of operation is similar to yours. For example, your project manager can be more effective if he or she has a clearly designated counterpart in the consultants office.
   e. Information on the consultant's specific computer software and hardware and other technical capabilities. It is important to have compatible software and systems. This is especially true if CADD systems are to be used to produce the work.
   f. A certificate of insurance indicating the existence of professional liability coverage and the amount. Failure to do so may leave you as the "deep pocket" in the event of a lawsuit.
   g. A summary of the potential consultant's quality control and assurance procedures. This will minimize client problems, contractor disagreements, and potential litigation.
5. Inform potential consultants of your methods of operation. If you have a project management manual, provide a copy for them as a reference guide to your operations. Require the return of this manual in the event the consultant is not selected.
6. Prepare a clear and complete contract. Never operate on a handshake or verbal agreement. This is especially true on change orders. Without effective change-order management, you may find your consultants undertaking work well beyond—or not in accord with—your client's wishes. Also, without a firm agreement on fees for changes, you may find the consultant invoicing you for an amount in excess of that which you will receive from the client.

Your agreement with outside consultants must be very specific on billing and payment terms and conditions. Many prime design firms are extremely slow to pay their consultants. The prime contractor must be prepared (under severe penalty) to pay consultants immediately after receiving payment from the client. This is a particularly upsetting subject to many engineers who work with architects. Some architects use money that rightfully should be paid to their engineers to finance their own poor management.

9

Federal Design Work

Many designers are familiar with the Federal Acquisition Regulations (FAR) regarding architect/engineer (A/E) selection. In brief, the FAR carry out the requirements of the Brooks Act (Public Law 92-582) that provide for the selection of the most highly qualified A/E firm on the basis of competence and at a fair and reasonable price. The FAR do not separately discuss selection procedures for open-ended or fixed-price contracts, but they are generally handled in the same manner.

On the other hand, most designers are unfamiliar with the internal procedures followed by a federal agency requiring A/E services. While procedures may differ somewhat in the various agencies, the methods are reasonably consistent. The process described here is drawn from the Public Health Service (PHS).

Preannouncement Actions

Request for new/changed facility

A representative of a local facility may request funding for changes or improvements to a building or for a new facility. Agency personnel also may determine a need. Whatever the source of the request, the process will require budgeting and appropriation action. In many cases, a 2- or 3-year lead time is required from request to appropriation.

For example, new construction requires the agency to submit a building and facilities plan by July 1 for inclusion in the budget request. July 1, 1992, was the deadline for inclusion in the fiscal year 1994 budget. Each agency establishes priorities of projects to be funded based on available appropriations.

Availability and certification of funds

The contract officer/specialist of the particular agency must determine that the funds for a requested project have been appropriated and apportioned. According to the PHS guidelines, "care must be taken to assure that the funds are sufficient to cover the design services and from appropriate funding source. Designs for new facilities, replacement facilities and building additions must be accomplished with funds appropriated for that specific project and designs for building improvement projects must normally be accomplished with such specifically designated funds or with lump sum amounts appropriated for repairs and improvements."

Occasionally, when time is critical, advertising for design services occurs before funding is actually received. This can happen only when the appropriation or apportionment is expected within 60 days. In these cases, the *Commerce Business Daily* (CBD) announcement must state that the awarding of the contract is subject to the receipt of funds.

Program of requirements (POR) document

The POR broadly defines, in architectural and engineering terms, the scope of the work. It is prepared by either a contract architect or engineer or by agency personnel specializing in A/E work prior to advertising in the CBD.

Preparation of the A/E statement of work

This document outlines the scope of services required of the submitting architects and/or engineers. It is prepared by the office responsible for the evaluation and selection of A/Es. If properly prepared, "it should avoid price negotiation problems, eliminate ambiguities and assure that the design will satisfy the program needs."

In some cases, the POR is incorporated into the statement of work. The POR, however, is usually a broad definition of work while the statement of work is a detailed analysis of the work required of the A/E.

Evaluation criteria

Before making a public announcement of the need for A/E services on a project, the agency must establish an evaluation criterion consistent with the Federal Acquisition Regulations. This criterion is then weighted according to the importance of each factor and is listed in the CBD announcement in descending order of importance.

Typical factors include:

- Qualifications of the project team such as team experience on similar projects and professional qualifications of the staff to be assigned to the project

- The A/E's ability and experience in the particular type of project requested by the agency

- The management ability and organization of the A/E firm, including factors such as the design firm's internal organization methods for project delivery, systems to maintain quality control, and cost and scheduling control

Government estimate of A/E costs

Regulations covering the preparation of an independent government estimated cost of A/E services are provided in FAR 36.605. This estimate is prepared prior to the issuance of a CBD announcement. It can be revised during the negotiation process with A/Es if the scope of work to be performed changes.

This estimate determines the adequacy of funding to cover the project as outlined in the statement of work. It also measures the fairness of an A/E's fee proposal. It is important for the agency official preparing the estimate to understand how A/Es operate and to be aware of industry standards, such as profit margins, salary costs, etc. The Brooks Act has set a statutory limit of A/E fees for basic design services at 6 percent of the estimated construction cost.

Government management plan

This plan is prepared concurrently with the government estimate of A/E fees and costs. It describes the "project team, individual responsibilities, relationships and interfaces. The project officer should indicate the major actions to be performed and indicate those responsible for the actions, on a bar or PERT-type chart, to facilitate the government in overseeing the flow of activity."

At this point, the agency is ready to make a public announcement of the planned A/E selection. Announcements for design contracts expected to exceed $10,000 must be published in the CBD. For those expected to be less than $10,000, "the notice may be publicized only in the area where the work is to be performed." Copies of the announcement are displayed in the local procuring office and (by law) in at least one local daily newspaper. Affected local professional societies sometimes are also notified. Many announcements appear in the CBD at least 30 days prior to the A/E selection.

The CBD announcement typically includes information about the project location, the services required, the importance of the major evaluation factors in descending order, range of construction cost, type of proposed contract, and estimated start and completion dates. Information on the deadline for responding must also be included.

The architect or engineer should provide a U.S. Government Agency Standard Form 254 (SF 254) with the submittal if one is not on file. An SF 255 will also be required. In addition, the agency may request additional material, such as brochures.

Postannouncement Selection Process

Most agencies have an A/E selection board to evaluate and negotiate with designers. Some agencies may need to establish a board to meet individual project requirements. Agencies typically collect and maintain data files on A/Es, including Standard Form 254 and other pertinent information. The SF 254 is kept on file for 1 year. It is important that design firms periodically send updated forms to agencies from whom they are interested in obtaining work. If this is done, firms will not need to resubmit an SF 254 with each response to a CBD announcement. The agency review board will examine current data from eligible firms, including those responding to the public announcement. The board will contact each responding firm if it requires additional information. Design firms that do not respond to this request within the allotted time will be dropped from further consideration.

Selection Procedures

Each board member typically reviews the submitted material and rates each A/E firm. Design firms are ranked from *most qualified* to *least qualified*. Rankings are compared and discussed if extreme variances have occurred. From these rankings, several (usually three) firms are selected for interviews.

After design firms have been selected for interviews, they are provided with copies of the statement of work and the program of requirements. At the interview, the designer should present the project management team, consultants, management plan for the project, key personnel, etc. Usually 2 to 3 weeks are provided to A/Es to prepare.

Each firm should be given the same amount of time for its interview. In practice, this may vary if a particular firm does not use all of its allotted time. After completion of the interviews, the members of the A/E selection board rank the firms again. These rankings are used to list the firms from most to least qualified. Typically, these rankings are forwarded to the appropriate contracting officer for follow-up and negotiation. The contracting officer begins with the highest-ranking design firm.

Negotiation Procedures

A letter is sent inviting the designer to submit a fee proposal that conforms to federal guidelines for allowable cost items. Designers must fully understand these guidelines. This letter outlines how the proposal is to be prepared and the date and time for submission of the proposal. A sample draft copy of a contract normally is included along with copies of joint venture agreements (if applicable). The letter should identify the type of contract that has been proposed and should give the name, address, and telephone number of the contact person for the designer if questions arise.

Large contracts may require special provisions. For example, if the proposal is expected to exceed $100,000, a preaward audit may be required prior to negotiations.

From the agency's point of view, the negotiation process is aimed at making certain that the A/E has a clear understanding of the project requirements and that the necessary personnel and facilities will be made available to complete the design portion of the project on time with a fair and reasonable price. The contracting officer is concerned that, as much as possible, the design solution be constructed within the government's cost estimate.

If a mutually satisfying contract cannot be negotiated with the highest-ranking firm, the contracting officer will obtain in writing a best and final offer. The officer will then terminate the negotiations and advise the design firm. Negotiations will start with the second-ranking firm and continue until a satisfactory conclusion is reached. If negotiations fail with all ranked firms, the process begins again with another announcement in the CBD.

Contract Award

With the selection of an A/E firm, the contracting officer prepares the necessary documents. These will reflect any changes made during the negotiations. These state the contract period, schedule, method of payment, etc.

Change Orders

Change orders are likely to occur during the life of the contract. The designer will make a written request to the agency's contract officer for a change. This request should include a fee proposal. After review and if approved, the contract will be modified by the contracting officer.

Chapter

10

Project Budgeting

The preparation of budgets and the monitoring of costs are major functions of project management. Although they are often performed separately, they are basic to a firm's profitability and success in providing effective professional services.

Budgeting Process

The project budgeting process has two interdependent aspects. They are: (1) estimating compensation before negotiating with the client and (2) determining the actual detailed project budget by project phase or activity. Neither can be adequately performed without the other.

Experience indicates that too many small design firms estimate compensation on a percentage of estimated construction cost basis, negotiate that fee with the client, and then attempt to fit their actual costs into that fee maximum. There are, of course, many other methods of job costing. These include time-based methods, such as straight time card and time card to a maximum. Others are task-based, such as fees based on average labor cost per sheet of drawings, while others may not have any real basis, such as those using a lump sum or a flat fee.

The preferred method is to determine a firm's actual costs first and then communicate the proposed fee to the client in whatever form required (percentage of construction cost, lump sum, cost plus, multiplier, or hourly rate). For example, Engineer Smith is competing against Engineer Jones for a commission. The prospective client has retained engineers in the past and has always negotiated a percentage of construction cost contract. Smith cannot present the prospect with an elaborate method of determining fair compensation if Jones simply offers a 5 percent fee to perform the work.

Smith's approach should be to determine actual costs while recording areas in which he has room to adjust his fee (perhaps by altering the scope of services he will provide). Then Smith should translate this fee into an estimated percentage of construction cost by the following formula:

$$\frac{\text{Smith's cost (including profit)}}{\text{Estimated construction costs}} = \text{Percent of construction cost (his fee)}$$

As mentioned, Jones has already set his fee at 5 percent. Suppose Smith's analysis results in a fee of 6 percent. His options are:

1. Alter the scope of services provided
2. Go with the 6 percent fee
3. Determine that his time is better spent seeking other projects that will provide the fee he desires
4. Take the project in the hope that he can complete it within the budget (without damaging quality and service)
5. Remind the client that a lower fee may mean lower service.

The decision is his. The key is knowing his costs.

Where do firms obtain the information to determine these actual costs? There are many sources including:

- The firm's experience and records on previous projects of similar scope (see Table 10.1, for suggested content for this historical file).

- Cost per sheet (sheet counts), only if this information is based on documented cost per sheet for services by project type. To use the cost per sheet from an old firm or a neighbor is not adequate. Cost must relate to the firm's level of productivity, projects, etc.

- A manager's knowledge of similar projects. This is often the single best source of data if combined with recorded historical information. In many firms the project manager's private files are often more complete than the firm's central files. With staff turnover, however, much of this information is often lost.

- Cost-based compensation guidelines (see Chap. 8). This system, developed by the AIA, provides an extensive breakdown of all possible services provided by a design firm. It is an excellent method to isolate the various activities you must perform and to determine a cost for each activity. Many firms have successfully used this system as an educational tool to show clients the multitude of tasks that are required to meet their needs. Figure 10.1 shows a sample budgeting form from this system. Full information on how to use the forms and procedures are contained in two AIA publications: *Compensation Guidelines for Architectural and Engineering Services* (2M188) and

TABLE 10.1   Supplementary Completed Project File

A single folder containing project information is required for each current job and each recently completed project.

Information required
Project Data

Project name
Project address
Related project references
Referenced contracts and addresses
Owner's name and address
Gross square footage
Construction costs
  Budgeted
  Contracted
  Final
Cost/gross square footage (exclusive of site work)
Cost analysis (if available)
Program summarization (major areas)
Fee
  Budgeted
  Final
Project starting date
Construction starting date
Final completion date
Final project summary report
Consultants (including addresses and telephone numbers)

Project Manager's Statement (one page)
Statement should cover the significance of the project, personnel involved, contractor selection process, scope of services, awards, information of public interest, potential of owner recommendation, etc.
Project Designer's Statement
Brief statement of the program, design constraints, objectives, materials, etc.
Copy of the Last Certificate of Payment, Including List of Contractors
List of Subcontractors and Material Suppliers
List should include product manufacturers for publication and field representatives' evaluation of each subcontractor and supplier (delivery time, quality of workmanship, recommendations for use on other projects, etc.).
Site Plan (8½ × 11 inches) Showing Building Configuration
One 8 × 10-inch Photo

PHASE COMPENSATION WORKSHEET

PHASE 5: CONSTRUCTION DOCUMENTS SERVICES

Project _____
Project # _____   Date _____
Owner _____
Architect _____

SERVICE	5.01 Project Administration	5.02 Disciplines Coord./ Document Checking	5.03 Agency Consulting/ Review/Approval	5.04 Owner-supplied Data Coordination	5.21 Architectural Design/ Documentation	5.22 Structural Design/ Documentation	5.23 Mechanical Design/ Documentation	5.24 Electrical Design/ Documentation	5.25 Civil Design/ Documentation	5.26 Landscape Design/ Documentation	5.27 Interior Design/ Documentation	5.28 Materials Research/ Specifications	5.30 Special Bidding Documents/Scheduling	5.32 Statement of Probable Construction Cost	5.33 Presentations	TOTAL HOURS	TOTAL DOLLARS	ITEM		LINE
IN-HOUSE PERSONNEL	Hrs. $																		@ $	1
	Hrs. $																		@ $	2
	Hrs. $																		@ $	3
	Hrs. $																		@ $	4
	Hrs. $																		@ $	5
SUB TOT.	Hrs. $																	Direct In-house Salary Expense		6
																		Direct Personnel Expense		7
																		Indirect Expense		8
																		Other Nonreimbursable Direct Expense		9
																		Total In-house Expense		10
OUT-SIDE	Hrs. $																	Outside Services Expense		11
TOT.	Hrs. $																	Estimated Total Expense		12
REMARKS																		Contingency		13
																		Profit		14
																		Proposed Compensation		15
																		Estimated Reimbursable Expense		16

Reproduced with permission of The American Institute of Architects under license number 91105. Permission expires August 1, 1992. FURTHER REPRODUCTION IS PROHIBITED.

Because AIA Documents are revised from time to time, users should ascertain from the AIA the current edition of this document. Copies of the current edition of this AIA document may be purchased from The American Institute of Architects or its local distributors.

The text of this document is not "model language" and is not intended for use in other documents without permission of the AIA.

AIA THE AMERICAN INSTITUTE OF ARCHITECTS
FM FINANCIAL MANAGEMENT SYSTEM

AIA® FORM FED5 · PHASE COMPENSATION WORKSHEET, PHASE 5 · JANUARY 1978 EDITION · © 1978
THE AMERICAN INSTITUTE OF ARCHITECTS, 1735 NEW YORK AVE., N.W., WASHINGTON, DC 20006

Figure 10.1 Sample completed phase compensation work sheet (form) F825. *(From Managing Architectural Projects: The Process, © 1984, The American Institute of Architects.)*

Compensation Management: A Guideline for Small Firms (2M737). (See Resources for more information). Both are available from local AIA bookstores or from the AIA in Washington [(202) 626-7300]. These forms integrate with AIA contract document number B161. Engineers and others can easily use the system and forms by simply changing the descriptions.

- Percentage of construction costs, only if it is based on the firm's actual recorded experience with the building type, with similar clients in similar locations, etc. This method may expose the firm to excessive loss if costs run higher than the fee or if the construction cost is reduced (either by redesign or low bids). At the same time, you should not try to make a windfall profit on a higher-than-anticipated construction cost.

Several other considerations are important in developing project budgets. Most designers neglect to forward-price their services. With inflation, the cost of labor and overhead will increase over the life of a project. Failure to anticipate these increases can easily turn a profit into a loss.

It is important to determine the level of service the firm can provide based on a client's needs and ability to pay. Clients with a greater ability to pay can receive more elaborate levels of service. Not all clients need to receive the same level of service.

The firm has to maintain quality and service but must know when the fee will not support even minimum standards and must be prepared to not seek the commission. To do otherwise is a disservice to the firm and to the potential client.

Project Cost Plan

A surprising number of firms do not have a formal method of developing a project budget. Often, for small projects, a detailed breakdown may not be necessary but the basic cost areas should be considered. All larger projects (even open-ended, time-card, or multiplier projects where an obligation to the client to control costs exists) should be controlled by a formal budget. The more successful firms often incorporate techniques to provide cross-checks using several budgeting methods.

Table 10.2 shows a project cost plan form incorporating a percent of construction cost cross-check (estimated construction cost). Other major sections include in-house services, direct (nonreimbursable) costs that come out of fees, profit, and reimbursable costs. This form is blank to permit copying for immediate use.

TABLE 10.2 Project Cost Plan

Scope of project:		Date: Project no.: Project name:

Estimated Construction Cost		
1. Site work	$	
2. General	$	
3. HVAC*	$	
4. Plumbing	$	
5. Electrical	$	
6. Kitchen	$	
7. Elevator	$	
8. Other	$	
Total	$	

Services Provided within the Firm		
1. Predesign	hours @ $/hour = $	
2. Site analysis	hours @ $/hour = $	
3. Schematic design	hours @ $/hour = $	
4. Design development	hours @ $/hour = $	
5. Construction documents	hours @ $/hour = $	
6. Bid/negotiation	hours @ $/hour = $	
7. Construction administration	hours @ $/hour = $	
8. Postconstruction	hours @ $/hour = $	
9. Supplementary services	hours @ $/hour = $	
Total labor	$	%
Overhead factor (%)	$	
Total labor and overhead	$	

Nonreimbursable Direct Costs (Costs That Come Out of Fee)		
1. Consultant 1	$	
2. Consultant 2	$	
3. Consultant 3	$	
4. Consultant 4	$	
5. Other consultants	$	
Subtotal consultants	$	%
6. Travel	$	
7. Reproduction and supplies	$	
8. Models and photographs	$	
9. Telephone and telegraph	$	
10. Other	$	
Subtotal nonreimbursables	$	%
Total nonreimbursable direct costs	$	

Profit		
1. Total labor, overhead, and direct	%	$
2. Contingency	%	$
3. Profit	__ %	$ _____
Total fee for service	100%	$
4. Markup on reimbursables fee quoted client		$ _____

Reimbursables		
1. Total (budgeted or by contract)	$	
Total compensation		$

TABLE 10.2   Project Cost Plan   (Continued)

Comments and Notes

*Heating, ventilating, and air conditioning.

Direct Personnel Expense   Unique to architectural firms is the use of the direct
personnel expense (DPE) factor. DPE bases the calculation of the hourly job cost
rate for an employee on raw labor plus all statutory and discretionary fringe
benefits. Statutory fringes such as state and federal unemployment insurance
taxes, the firm's portion of social security, and worker's compensation insurance
are paid by virtually all design firms. The level of these, however, varies greatly
by location. Discretionary fringes include: major medical insurance, long-term
disability insurance, dental insurance, life insurance, vacation, sick leave, hol-
iday pay, and a great variety of other benefits. Not only the components of the
DPE factor, but also the levels of each, vary from firm to firm and among employees of the same firm.

The use of DPE factors has long been incorporated in standard American Institute of Architects contract forms. Typically, the DPE factor is multiplied by a
factor   that   covers   non-fringe-benefit   overhead   expenses,   profit,   and
nonreimbursable (direct) consultant and nonconsultant expenses. Most other design professionals simply multiply raw labor by a factor that includes all overhead costs such as fringes, profit, and nonreimbursable (direct) expenses. Raw
labor is defined as *the dollar amount job-costed to a project even if it is different
than the employee's actual pay rate.*

In nearly all cases, a firm using a DPE factor as a base will have what appears
to be a lower multiplier. This may be of great value to a firm in a price-
competitive situation trying to provide—or give the illusion of—a lower multiplier. (The use of a multiplier is particularly significant in time-card or time-
card-to-a-maximum contracts.)

This edge, however, may only be illusory. It is very possible that a firm using
a DPE base may actually have a higher multiplier than a firm using raw labor.
For example, firm A has a DPE factor of 1.4 (if raw labor is a dollar, then fringes
are another 40 cents) and a multiplier for nonreimbursables, profit, and overhead of 2.5 times DPE. Firm B has a raw labor rate of 1.0 and a multiplier of 3.2
times raw labor. Firm A appears to have the lower multiplier (2.5 versus 3.2),
but on closer examination, firm A's multiplier is actually 3.5 (1.4 × 2.5). To the
unaware client, firm A appears to be less expensive, while the reverse is actually true.

In a competitive situation, wise negotiators present their firms in the best
possible light. Translating and presenting a cost structure to a potential client
using DPE could be to the firm's advantage. Significant problems can be cre-

ated, however, if the firm attempts to use DPE-based data for internal management and permanent records. With the fringe benefit mix varying from employee to employee, project to project, and period to period, the firm's management is never certain (without extensive research) of the actual base labor dollars required and the actual cost of doing the project. DPE-based records are nearly useless for building vitally important historical databases because even averages are rendered meaningless by a changing package of fringe benefits. By removing fringes from overhead and including them in the DPE factor charged (usually this is done by calculating a firmwide fringe factor to be added to raw labor), the actual overhead cost associated with a project can be distorted. Some firms avoid this distortion by providing each employee with a personal fringe factor. Extensive research would still be required, however, to make use of the firm's database. The best solution is to keep all records on a raw-labor basis and provide clients with an equivalent DPE multiplier only when competitive conditions make it necessary.

Tables 10.3 through 10.7 trace the development of a hypothetical project budget.

Using detailed work sheets, client input, previous experience, and other methods, a general estimate of construction costs by major area is developed. This estimate is then used to determine an estimated fee based on the firm's historical percentage of construction cost database. The estimate is used only as a cross-check with other methods of estimating compensation.

Services provided within the firm are determined by a careful analysis of the scope of the project (Table 10.4). (The breakdown of services shown is for illustration only.) Hours to complete each task are estimated and multiplied by the average raw labor rate (*not* direct personnel expense factor—labor plus fringes) of all individuals who will be working on that phase. Each of these line items is totaled to obtain the total labor amount of $2612 shown.

TABLE 10.3   Project Cost Plan—Part 1

Scope of project:
  Provide complete design services for
  City Hall alterations
	Date: November 30, 1992
	Project no.: 02792
	Project name:
	City Hall alterations
	Any City, Texas

Estimated Construction Cost		
1. Site work	$25,000	
2. General	$80,000	
3. HVAC	$40,000	
4. Plumbing	$10,000	
5. Electrical	$10,000	
6. Kitchen	$ 5,000	
7. Elevator	$20,000	
8. Other	$10,000	
Total		$200,000

TABLE 10.4   Project Cost Plan—Part 2

Scope of project: Provide complete design services for City Hall alterations	Date: November 30, 1992 Project no.: 02792 Project name: City Hall alterations Any City, Texas

Estimate Construction Cost (Sample Breakdown Only)		
1. Site work	$25,000	
2. General	$80,000	
3. HVAC	$40,000	
4. Plumbing	$10,000	
5. Electrical	$10,000	
6. Kitchen	$ 5,000	
7. Elevator	$20,000	
8. Other	$10,000	
Total		$200,000

Services Provided within the Firm (Sample Breakdown Only)		
1. Predesign	20 hours @ 10 $/hour = $200	
2. Site analysis	4 hours @ 8 $/hour = $ 32	
3. Schematic design	20 hours @ 15 $/hour = $300	
4. Design development	30 hours @ 12 $/hour = $360	
5. Construction documents	88 hours @ 10 $/hour = $880	
6. Bid/negotiation	10 hours @ 12 $/hour = $120	
7. Construction administration	40 hours @ 18 $/hour = $720	
8. Postconstruction	— hours @ — $/hour = —	
9. Supplementary services	— hours @ — $/hour = —	
Total labor	$2612	
Overhead factor (150%)	$3918	
Total labor and overhead		$6530

Revealing Salary Information to Project Managers   Some design firm principals are reluctant to provide salary data to project managers. This is done in the mistaken belief that the confidentiality of pay rates is being protected. Unfortunately, this places an unfair burden on project managers. They are expected to manage costs on projects without knowing what they are.

You cannot manage a project by using hours alone. It is extremely likely that meeting the hours budget will result in a dollar amount at great variance with the budget. This occurs because the mix of individuals actually working on a project and their pay rates is often at great variance with that in mind when a fee is negotiated. Managing on hours fails to provide the project manager any frame of reference for controlling project costs.

Some design firms have pay rates that differ from the employees' actual job cost rate. Standardized employee classifications may exist, such as Technical I and Technical II, where all workers in a class are job-costed at the same rate.

In other firms, job cost rates are rounded to the nearest $1 or $10 to promote standardization or to ease budgeting and management. Both result in a variance from pay rates. In these cases, the PM does not need to know pay rates, but only job cost rates. However, senior firm managers must recognize that this variance will make it more difficult for project managers to effectively control costs.

The firm's overhead is determined by multiplying labor by an overhead factor (in this example, it is 150 percent). Hence, the overhead factor line is calculated by the following:

$$\$2612 \times 150\%(1.5) = \$3918$$

Total labor and overhead is determined by adding $2612 and $3918 to equal $6530.

Table 10.5 adds project-related nonreimbursable direct costs that come out of the fee. The consultant cost budget should be determined by written agreement with each consultant. Other nonreimbursable direct costs should be determined by a careful analysis of expected costs. All costs in this section should be kept to a minimum because those costs reduce potential profit for the firm. As shown in Table 10.5, nonreimbursable direct costs total $2600.

Reimbursable Markups Many design firms mark up reimbursables. The typical markup is 10 percent, with a range from 5 to 25 percent. Often, firms attempt to justify this markup by claiming that they are incurring additional administrative, clerical, and coordination time (direct labor time by technical staff and project managers) and expense in processing these items. This claim is often difficult to substantiate, since these costs are normally charged to overhead. If they are being charged to clients as a markup, then the overhead rate charged should be reduced accordingly. Failure to do so will result in double-charging clients for the same item. If the time and expense being incurred in processing these items is extreme, they should be charged as a direct project cost and not as a markup or overhead.

There are, however, situations where a markup is justified. A firm's opportunity cost of money tied up in paying for reimbursables prior to payment by the client is a justified charge. For example, if a firm could earn 6 percent interest on money in an investment account, but instead must use it to pay reimbursable vendor bills, or jeopardize its own credit standing, there is an opportunity cost incurred.

A firm also incurs a real cost when it must borrow money to pay for reimbursable vendor bills for a slow-paying client. When clients are willing to provide a retainer or other guarantee of prompt payment, a markup can be eliminated.

Lastly, an argument could be made for charging a markup on an item to avoid raising the firm's cost structure and penalizing all of your clients. For example, a particularly large project may significantly increase your professional liability premium. This may result in raising your overhead rate, thus making you more expensive to all your current and potential clients. By directly charging the responsible client for this cost, perhaps by treating it as a reimbursable item with a markup, you avoid this problem.

In cases where clients, in the negotiation process, refuse to allow you a sufficient overhead rate to cover actual costs,you are justified in seeking a markup to cover the clearly identifiable costs of processing reimbursables. It is most important, however, that the firm's negotiators completely understand their cost structure. Markups should not be established simply because competitors are doing so or because an unaware client permits it. Markups must be justified to be valid.

TABLE 10.5   Project Cost Plan—Part 3

Scope of project: Provide complete design services for City Hall alterations	Date: November 30, 1992 Project no.: 02792 Project name: City Hall alterations Any City, Texas

Estimated Construction Cost		
1. Site work	$25,000	
2. General	$80,000	
3. HVAC	$40,000	
4. Plumbing	$10,000	
5. Electrical	$10,000	
6. Kitchen	$ 5,000	
7. Elevator	$20,000	
8. Other	$10,000	
Total		$200,000

Services Provided within the Firm (Sample Breakdown Only)	
1. Predesign	20 hours @ 10 $/hour = $200
2. Site analysis	4 hours @ 8 $/hour = $ 32
3. Schematic design	20 hours @ 15 $/hour = $300
4. Design development	30 hours @ 12 $/hour = $360
5. Construction documents	88 hours @ 10 $/hour = $880
6. Bid/negotiation	10 hours @ 12 $/hour = $120
7. Construction administration	40 hours @ 18 $/hour = $720
8. Postconstruction	— hours @ — $/hour = —
9. Supplementary Services	— hours @ — $/hour = —
Total labor	$2612
Overhead factor (150%)	$3918
Total labor and overhead	$6,530

Nonreimbursable Direct Costs (Costs That Come Out of Fee)		
1. Consultant 1	$ 800	
2. Consultant 2	$ 600	
3. Consultant 3	$ 600	
4. Consultant 4	$ —	
5. Other consultants	$ 400	
Subtotal consultants	$ 2,400	
6. Travel	$ —	
7. Reproduction, supplies, and printing	$ 100	
8. Models and photographs	$ 50	
9. Telephone and telegraph	$ 30	
10. Other	$ 20	
Subtotal nonreimbursables	$200	
Total nonreimbursable direct costs		$2,600

Too often, profit is considered the amount left over when the project is complete. Profit should be planned for as shown in Table 10.6. The first step is to determine costs by adding together total labor, overhead, and nonreimbursable direct costs:

Total labor	$2612
Overhead factor	3918
Direct costs	2600
Total	$9130

To this total add factors for contingencies (3 percent is a generally accepted standard) and profit (17 to 20 percent is generally targeted). Hence,

$$3\% \times \$9130 = \$274$$

$$17\% \times \$9130 = \$1552$$

Thus, the total fee for services is

$$\$9130 + \$274 + \$1552 = \$10,956$$

Note that if the calculation for profit is made by first determining a total fee for services (perhaps on a percentage of construction cost), and then taking 17 percent for profit (off the top), the dollar amount for profit would be much different:

$$\$10,956 \times 17\% = \$1863$$

Compare this amount with the $1552 determined by the cost-based method ($311 less). The result is a higher profit budget but a lower amount available to budget for other items. But this is trying to fit a square peg in a round hole. The cost-based method is preferred because it determines profit from the actual cost of doing the work and not from an artificially remaining amount after profit is deducted.

The final items to consider are reimbursable expenses over and above the basic fee for service. These expenses are developed from a separate schedule. A percentage markup (often ranging from 5 to 25 percent) sometimes is added to this amount called "Reimbursable Markups" (also see page 80). In Table 10.7 total reimbursable expenses are $3000 and the markup on these reimbursables is $544 or about 18 percent. Reimbursables include many of the same types of items (including consultants) shown under direct costs. Hence, a line item for a soils consultant may be found under both the direct and reimbursable sections as well(the same is true for other items) depending on the contract with the client.

This completes the basics of project budgeting. After determining the actual costs, a fee may be presented to the client in whatever form desired. To adjust the fee, modify the relevant section of the project cost plan and revise the subsequent figures.

TABLE 10.6   **Project Cost Plan—Part 4**

Scope of project: Provide complete design services for City Hall alterations	Date: November 30, 1992 Project no.: 02792 Project name: City Hall alterations Any City, Texas

Estimated Construction Cost		
1. Site work	$25,000	
2. General	$80,000	
3. HVAC	$40,000	
4. Plumbing	$10,000	
5. Electrical	$10,000	
6. Kitchen	$ 5,000	
7. Elevator	$20,000	
8. Other	$10,000	
Total		$200,000

Services Provided within the Firm (Sample Breakdown Only)		
1. Predesign	20 hours @ 10 $/hour = $200	
2. Site analysis	4 hours @ 8 $/hour = $ 32	
3. Schematic design	20 hours @ 15 $/hour = $300	
4. Design development	30 hours @ 12 $/hour = $360	
5. Construction documents	88 hours @ 10 $/hour = $880	
6. Bid/negotiation	10 hours @ 12 $/hour = $120	
7. Construction administration	40 hours @ 18 $/hour = $720	
8. Postconstruction	— hours @ — $/hour = —	
9. Supplementary services	— hours @ — $/hour = —	
Total labor	$2612	
Overhead factor (150%)	$3918	
Total labor and overhead		$6,530

Nonreimbursable Direct Costs (Costs That Come Out of Fee)		
1. Consultant 1	$ 800	
2. Consultant 2	$ 600	
3. Consultant 3	$ 600	
4. Consultant 4	$ —	
5. Other consultants	$ 400	
Subtotal consultants	$ 2400	
6. Travel	$ —	
7. Reproduction, supplies, and printing	$ 100	
8. Models and photographs	$ 50	
9. Telephone and telegraph	$ 30	
10. Other	$ 20	
Subtotal nonreimbursables	$ 200	
Total nonreimbursable direct costs		$2,600

Profit			
1. Total labor, overhead, and direct	80%	$9130	
2. Contingency	3%	274	
3. Profit	17%	1552	
Total fee for services	100%		$10,956
4. Markup on reimbursables		$544	
Fee quoted client			$11,500

TABLE 10.7 Project Cost Plan—Part 5

Scope of project: Provide complete design services for City Hall alterations	Date: November 30, 1992 Project no.: 02792 Project name: City Hall alterations Any City, Texas

Estimated Construction Cost		
1. Site work	$25,000	
2. General	$80,000	
3. HVAC	$40,000	
4. Plumbing	$10,000	
5. Electrical	$10,000	
6. Kitchen	$ 5,000	
7. Elevator	$20,000	
8. Other	$10,000	
Total		$200,000

Services Provided within the Firm (Sample Breakdown Only)		
1. Predesign	20 hours @ 10 $/hour = $200	
2. Site analysis	4 hours @ 8 $/hour = $ 32	
3. Schematic design	20 hours @ 15 $/hour = $300	
4. Design development	30 hours @ 12 $/hour = $360	
5. Construction documents	88 hours @ 10 $/hour = $880	
6. Bid/negotiation	10 hours @ 12 $/hour = $120	
7. Construction administration	40 hours @ 18 $/hour = $720	
8. Postconstruction	— hours @ — $/hour = —	
9. Supplementary services	— hours @ — $/hour = —	
Total labor	$2612	
Overhead factor (150%)	$3918	
Total labor and overhead		$6,530

Nonreimbursable Direct Costs (Costs That Come Out of Fee)		
1. Consultant 1	$ 800	
2. Consultant 2	$ 600	
3. Consultant 3	$ 600	
4. Consultant 4	$ —	
5. Other consultants	$ 400	
Subtotal consultants	$ 2,400	
6. Travel	$ —	
7. Reproduction, supplies, and printing	$ 100	
8. Models and photographs	$ 50	
9. Telephone and telegraph	$ 30	
10. Other	$ 20	
Subtotal nonreimbursables	$ 200	
Total nonreimbursable direct costs		$2,600

Profit			
1. Total labor, overhead, and direct	80%	$9,130	
2. Contingency	3%	274	
3. Profit	17%	1,552	
Total fee for services	100%		$10,956
4. Markup on reimbursables		$ 544	
Fee quoted client			$11,500

Reimbursables		
1. Total (budgeted or by contract)	$3,000	
Total compensation		$14,500

11

Project
Scheduling

Project schedules are important and highly useful tools for designers. The preparation of schedules allows for detailed planning of work activities and provides a device for communicating critical dates and activities to clients, consultants, and the internal project team. In addition, schedules provide a tool to help program the project, test alternative approaches, and evaluate job performance.

The development of a project schedule is an aid—not a substitute for project management. It is a useful method for monitoring percentage of project complete, offers guideposts for the project team, and can show the real possibility of meeting deadlines.

The first step in developing a project schedule begins with defining the planning units. These may be based on geography (locations), function (architect, engineer, etc.) or phase (design, construction documents, etc.). Second, decisions must be made as to the kinds of information a schedule should show. This may be simply a list of activities to be accomplished or may include time frames, sequences, and individuals responsible.

Scheduling Methods

An appropriate scheduling method must be selected and prepared in written form. While many computer programs are available to accomplish this step, care must be exercised not to make the schedule overly complicated. As a communication tool, it must be presented in a clear enough manner to achieve its primary purpose.

Many scheduling methods exist, and each has its own strengths and weaknesses. Several such methods are

Full wall scheduling

This is a somewhat antiquated method by which project tasks are listed, the individual responsible for each is noted and a preliminary schedule prepared. The tasks are listed on 3 × 5-inch index cards and divided into piles for each responsible party. The list of individuals is posted on one side of an office wall and the time frames or periods are listed along the top of the wall. All participants are assembled and the tasks are tacked to the wall according to when the activity will be started and finished. In this method, a schedule is developed and all participants understand their own responsibilities.

The disadvantages of this method are many. To be most effective, all parties (including the client, consultants, contractor, etc.) must be available to participate in the planning session. On large projects, this can be an extremely time-consuming process. An advantage is that it allows a high degree of interaction between all project participants at an early stage of the job.

Bar charts

This is a time-tested and familiar device for scheduling. A bar chart shows a list of activities, the responsible party and the duration of an activity. Bar charts are easy to prepare, are familiar to most people, and clearly communicate information. (See example in "Critical path method" section of this chapter.) In addition, they are excellent and simple tools for monitoring. Other methods, however, are superior for planning purposes.

Bar charts do have several disadvantages. They do not show sequencing of events/activities and the interrelationship among tasks. In addition, on a bar chart every task appears equal in importance.

Critical path method*

The critical path method is perhaps the most widely used scheduling method. The network schedule has its ancestry in the bar chart. The inadequacies of this method resulted, in 1956, in motivating the DuPont Company to adopt the rapidly growing power of the computer to construction scheduling. The system they developed is called the *critical path method* (CPM).

---

*The remainder of the material in this chapter was prepared by Tom Eyerman, FAIA, and is taken from his *Financial Management Concepts and Techniques for the Architect* (see Bibliography).

At about the same time, the U.S. Navy developed a system called Program Evaluation and Review Technique (PERT). The primary difference between the two is that CPM uses one time estimate and PERT uses three (most likely, optimistic, and pessimistic).

Many CPM and PERT applications in the construction process occur during the actual construction phase. The networks that are developed can range from less than 100 to many thousands of activities. It is the development of a disciplined method of planning sequences that is important in CPM and PERT, not simply the use of the computer. Not only is the planning process significant with this method, but it also encourages the effective management of schedules.

In developing a CPM schedule, the project manager must identify the interrelationships between tasks and establish their duration. The PM must prepare a schedule of activities and determine the critical paths or steps.

The first and most important step in preparing a project for networking is the correct division of the job into units of work that are relevant to the people for whom it is being prepared. For example, a network indicating just three subjects—design, working drawings, and construction—may be applicable for the design professional to show a client. For internal use, however, each of these subjects might be subdivided—for example, working drawings into architectural, mechanical, and structural drawings. Furthermore, to be of any aid to the architectural job captain, the drawings might be subdivided into plans, sections, and elevations. Networks for internal control must be developed at the level where the work is to be performed. Once the network process is removed from the operation level, it becomes merely a theoretical tool. No matter how detailed and accurate a network may be, if it is not meaningful to the user, it is useless. The personal involvement of these people is what makes a network a viable tool.

The level at which the designer wants a network, commonly called the level of indenture, is determined by "Who is it for?" and "What is its purpose?" Answers to these two questions are the first management decisions in developing a network.

Once the level of indenture has been established, each division of work is split into a number of component parts called activities. An activity is any definable time-consuming task necessary to execute a project. An example of an activity is drawing wall sections.

A network has three phases:

- *Planning* is the study or recognition of the events and their interrelationships that are necessary to complete a project. A network is a systematic attempt to plan the work. Just as a wall section shows how a wall is to be built, the network is a graphic representation of how the project will be produced in the office. The people performing this task must have a sound knowledge of how a job is put together. Moreover, they must have a thorough understanding of the particular project and of the scope involved.

- *Scheduling* is the second phase of networking. A reasonable estimate is made of the time required to perform each event shown on the network developed in the planning stage. With the network and the estimated time for each activity, you can proceed in an entirely mechanical manner to determine the overall time required for a project. By establishing the time required, the design professional is establishing the budget for the project. Just as dimensions on a wall section tell how high the structure will be, the schedule tells how long it will take to produce the project.

- *Monitoring* is the third phase of networking. Monitoring means nothing more than comparing what is actually being done with what was planned. In other words, "We have planned the work, now we work the plan." The network enables you to spot difficulties at an early stage of the project. This is the point where the accounting reports must tie in with the network.

The start and completion of an activity is called an *event*. An event is a specific point in time indicating the beginning or ending of one or more activities. An example of an event is *wall sections completed*. An example of an activity is *preparing wall section of exterior wall*.

In preparing a project for networking, it is most useful to define the last event and then work backward from that point. As the activities and events are developed, they are plotted on a piece of paper to create a pictorial description of the network. An activity is represented by an arrow; an event is represented by a circle. PERT is generally event-oriented, and CPM is activity-oriented.

Events and activities must be sequenced on the network under a logical set of ground rules which allow the determination of critical paths. These ground rules are shown in Table 11.1.

In example 5, X is called a dummy variable. It represents a restraint (halting start of activity C until activity B is completed) which cannot be recognized by the conventional symbols for events and activities.

How can networking techniques represent activities which are shown in a Gantt (bar) chart as illustrated in Fig. 11.1? The answer is that there must be something which causes the decision to start an activity. The task of the person developing the network is to isolate this decision-causing point and to include it as an event on the network. In the preceding example, the decision to start construction of A is determined by approval of the design for A.

TABLE 11.1

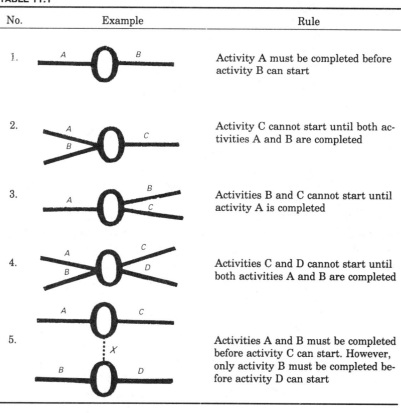

No.	Example	Rule
1.		Activity A must be completed before activity B can start
2.		Activity C cannot start until both activities A and B are completed
3.		Activities B and C cannot start until activity A is completed
4.		Activities C and D cannot start until both activities A and B are completed
5.		Activities A and B must be completed before activity C can start. However, only activity B must be completed before activity D can start

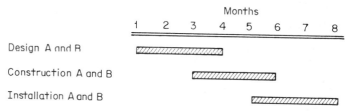

Figure 11.1 Gantt chart.

Figure 11.2 shows a sample network for solution of the problem. When the network is completed, an estimate is made as to how long each particular activity will take.

A further development in networking can be to calculate the earliest and latest time an event can take place without affecting the completion of the project's final event. The difference between the earliest and latest time an event could occur is called *slack time*.

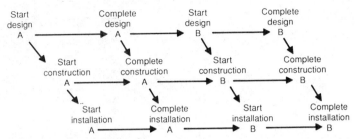

Figure 11.2 Sample network.

The critical path is then simply the series of activities and events that have no slack time. The critical path, therefore, is the bottleneck route. Only by finding ways to shorten jobs along the critical path can the overall project time be reduced; the time required to perform noncritical jobs is irrelevant from the viewpoint of total project time. The frequent (and costly) practice of "crashing" all jobs in a project in order to reduce total project time is thus unnecessary. Of course, if some way is found to shorten one or more of the critical jobs, then not only will the whole project time be shortened, but the critical path itself may shift and some previously noncritical jobs may become critical.

Once the network is developed and the critical path established, cost estimates are made by first determining the personnel to perform each activity. The personnel allocation is then converted to dollars to determine the direct cost of the activity. These cost estimates are used in three ways:

1. To aid the professional in determining a fee

2. To evaluate overall the project in terms of expenses before any action is taken

3. To provide benchmarks against which actual costs can be compared

This then describes the networking technique. A single example should help to clarify the process of constructing a network. The example project of building a house is taken from "ABC's of the Critical Path Method" by F. K. Levy, G. L. Thompson, and J. D. West, *Harvard Business Review*, September–October, 1963.

Table 11.2 shows a list of major tasks together with estimated time and the immediate predecessors for each task.

By following the ground rules for networking, the network in Fig. 11.3 can be developed. The path A-B-C-D-J-K-L-N-T-U-X is the critical path, with a maximum of 34 days.

TABLE 11.2

Task no.	Immediate predecessors and description		Normal time, days
A		Start	0
B	a	Excavate and pour footers	4
C	b	Pour concrete foundation	2
D	c	Erect wooden frame including rough roof	4
E	d	Lay brickwork	6
F	c	Install basement drains and plumbing	1
G	f	Pour basement floor	2
H	f	Install rough plumbing	3
I	d	Install rough wiring	2
J	d, g	Install heating and ventilating	4
K	i, j, h	Fasten plasterboard and plaster (including drying)	10
L	k	Lay finish flooring	3
M	l	Install kitchen fixtures	1
N	l	Install finish plumbing	2
O	l	Finish carpentry	3
P	e	Finish roofing and flashing	2
Q	p	Fasten gutters and downspouts	1
R	c	Lay storm drains for rainwater	1
S	o, t	Sand and varnish flooring	2
T	m, n	Paint	3
U	t	Finish electrical work	1
V	q, r	Finish grading	2
W	v	Pour walks and complete landscaping	5
X	s, u, w	Finish	0

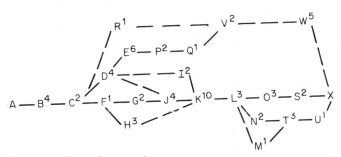

Figure 11.3 Example network.

Suppose now that October 1 is the target time for completing the project. This date is subtracted from the time for event X and the remaining time is forwarded to event S. Assuming a 6-day work period, you can see that event A must be started no later than August 23. Using the same analysis, you can see that event V may start as early as September 13 or as late as September 24.

Benefits and Limitations

The benefits of using a network are:

1. A network gives the architect or engineer a method of programming the project and then a method of evaluating the office performance during the project and not after the project is completed.

2. A network provides a plan that can be distributed to the project team so they know where they are headed and how they are going to get there. Furthermore, a network, by indicating a percent of completion for various calendar days, provides the professional with a good check on the actual percent of completion. Everyone on the project team knows what must be completed by a certain date. Thus, rather than look at a completion date several months in the future, they direct their attention to what they must accomplish in the next 2-week period.

3. A network is an excellent tool to show current and potential clients what must happen in the office to produce a set of drawings. It may help the client reach a decision quickly, knowing the completion date may be extended a month because of indecision; also a network can show very early in the project whether the scheduled client dates can be made. Thus the design professional is able to give the client realistic dates of completion while avoiding the embarrassing task of explaining to an owner why the contract documents will not be finished on time.

4. The network may be used to determine what fee is actually necessary to perform the work a client demands.

5. A network gives the designer a basis to determine the future personnel requirements for the office. The networks will never give an exact personnel projection since there are always small jobs which occur that take personnel, but are too small to network. With experience, however, the professional should be able to project fairly accurate personnel requirements.

6. A framework is developed which can be used to test out alternative approaches to a project.

The benefits described above do not just happen. The designer must become involved with, support, and use the network. But in order to do this you must be able to:

1. Fully define the project to a point where events and activities are clearly expressed

2. Keep the size and complexity of the network reasonable

3. Have your employees cooperate in developing a meaningful network

In summary, networking cannot be delegated to a clerk; rather it requires active support and judgment of the project manager.

There are certain limitations of networking:

1. Networking is not a panacea for ineffective management. It is an improvement over other project planning devices such as Gantt charts. It also allows for the generation of analytical information that was not previously available.

2. The introduction of networking will probably increase costs. Consequently, the cost of introducing networking into a specific situation must be evaluated against the increased benefits received from the additional information that may be available. This evaluation will by no means always favor networking.

3. Networks have caused some people to look backward, seeking to place or shift the blame for lack of progress rather than look forward seeking to bring the project to a successful conclusion.

For many networking applications, simple personal-computer-based software is available. This makes the use and benefits of network scheduling available to all design firms.

Many excellent texts are available for guidance in developing a network schedule. One of the best is *CPM in Construction Management* by James J. O'Brien (see Resources for more information).

Other Methods

There are numerous other scheduling methods in common use. The milestone chart shows activities, duration, and start and finish dates. Others include the cumulative graph, histogram, and project chart. All have their uses and applications.

Managing
the Project

12

Project Status Reporting

A significant number of small design firms fail to monitor project costs adequately. This failure works to the detriment of firms in several ways:

1. They lose control over current projects because they do not know the amount of money spent versus the amount budgeted, money spent to date, and other key financial factors.

2. They fail to build a historical base of information to use for future fee negotiations and project budgeting.

3. As a result, they are unable to develop management reports to analyze problem areas in the firm.

4. They lack documentation to support claims for additional compensation.

Tables 12.1 to 12.5 illustrate the development of a basic project status reporting system. The first step in developing a reporting system involves formulating a method of allocating direct labor and expenses by project. Labor is distributed by using a labor cost sheet (Table 12.1), which is prepared each time-card period and includes only labor charges made in that period. Some firms alter this form by listing the phase first, then the employee. The invoice code dates when the item is invoiced (most useful in a manual system).

Project-related direct and reimbursable expenses can be recorded by the method shown in Table 12.2. This report is normally prepared each month and includes only expenses paid (or accrued) that month. The invoice code dates when the item is invoiced.

TABLE 12.1   Labor Cost Sheet

Project name: City Hall alterations

Project no.: 02792

Period: November 1–30, 1992

Employee name	Phase	Hours	Rate, $	Job cost amount, $	Invoice code
Jones, R.	SD	3	12	36	
Doe, W.		2	10	20	
Clark, H.		1	8	8	
Total phase		6		64	
Jones, R.	DD	4	12	48	
Total phase		4		48	
Total project		10		112	Billed 12/2/92

NOTE: SD = schematic design; DD = design development.

TABLE 12.2   Project Expense Sheet

Project name: City Hall alterations

Project no.: 02792

Period: November 1–30, 1992

	Nonreimbursable Direct Expenses			
Item	Vendor	Date	Amount, $	Comments
Consultants				
	Dawson Consultants	11/05	$250	
	Doe Planners	11/08	100	
Total consultants			$350	
Travel				
	United Airlines	11/10	$195	
Total travel			$195	
Total nonreimbursable direct expenses			$545	

	Reimbursable Expenses			
Item	Vendor	Date	Amount, $	Invoice code
Consultants				
	Harris Design	11/15	$150	
	Stanley Survey	11/18	50	
Total consultants			$200	
Printing				
	Robinsons Printers	11/12	$ 25	
Total printing			$ 25	
Total reimbursable expenses			$225	Billed 12/2/92
Total expenses			$770	

Project Summary Report

Direct labor

The information contained on the labor cost sheet and the project expense sheet is used to assemble a monthly (or bimonthly) project summary report as shown in Tables 12.3 to 12.5.

Daily Time Sheets A good idea from Australian architect Rob Herriot:
I have a suggestion for your readers. Why not use daily time sheets? We changed over to daily time cards some years ago and have had a special computer program written to manage the time cost system in our office.
Daily time cards make it even harder to lose time. This is very important from both a costing and charging point of view. The time cards are collected (or demanded) for all staff at 9:00 a.m. each morning and are immediately entered into the computer. Any extra time and effort is more than made up for by the otherwise forgotten time left off time sheets.
With professional time billable at such a high rate, you don't have to save much time to be a long way in front. You also minimize the risk of inaccurate (or faked) time sheets and can more carefully evaluate the productivity of individual staff members.

The direct labor portion of the report contains three sections:

1. Current period hours and dollars from the labor cost sheet
2. Project-to-date cumulative hours and dollars from the project's inception
3. The budget as determined on the project cost plan

TABLE 12.3   Project Summary Report

Project name: City Hall alterations   Project no.: 02792

Period: November 1–30, 1992

Compensation schedule: Principal: Jones   Project manager: Doe
$14,500* maximum

| | Direct Labor | | | | | |
| | Current period | | Project to date | | Budget | |
Phase	Hours	Dollars	Hours	Dollars	Hours	Dollars
SD (including predesign)	6	64	8	80	74	692
DD	4	48	4	48	40	280
CD	—	—	—	—	160	800
BN	—	—	—	—	10	120
CA	—	—	—	—	90	720
Total labor	10	112	12	128	374	2612

*From project cost plan.
NOTE: SD = schematic design
DD = design development
CD = construction documents
BN = bidding negotiating
CA = construction administration

All labor dollars are without fringes. Principals' time and all direct labor hours are job-costed at an established rate for all projects. Typically, this is accomplished by dividing annual salary (or in the case of principals, a salary draw) by 2080 hours (52 weeks × 40 hours per week). Thus, an employee paid $20,800 per year would be job-costed as follows:

$$\frac{20,800}{2080} = \$10 \text{ per hour}$$

Hourly employees are generally costed at their hourly pay rate. (There are many other ways of establishing job cost rates. However, this is the basic method.)

Overhead

Table 12.4 illustrates the addition of overhead to the labor spent to date. Prior to November 1, only 2 hours and $16 were spent on this project. It was budgeted at 150 percent overhead (multiple of labor). Hence, it is assumed that prior to November 1 the firm's actual overhead was 150 percent. Thus the prior period overhead allocation is calculated as

$$\$16 \times 1.5 \,(150\%) = \$24.00$$

Current period overhead is calculated at $112 (current period

TABLE 12.4   Project Summary Report

Project name: City Hall alterations   Project no.: 02792

Period: November 1–30, 1992

Compensation schedule: $14,500* maximum	Principal: Jones		Project manager: Doe			
		Direct Labor				
	Current period		Project to date		Budget	
Phase	Hours	Dollars	Hours	Dollars	Hours	Dollars
SD (including predesign)	6	64	8	80	74	692
DD	4	48	4	48	40	280
CD	—	—	—	—	160	800
BN	—	—	—	—	10	120
CA	—	—	—	—	90	720
Total labor	10	112	12	128	374	2612

Overhead allocation (current factor: 152%)
Prior balance: $ 24
Current period: 170
Project to date: $194   3918

labor) × the November overhead rate of 152 percent, or $112 × 1.52 = $170.24. The resulting total overhead allocation to date is $24.00 + $170.24 = $194.24. The current period overhead rate is not multiplied by all labor spent to date, since the overhead rate may have been different in previous periods (as in the example). Multiplying by all labor spent would be misleading for management purposes and would misstate (in this case overstate) the total overhead allocation.

The overhead rate is determined by taking the firm's total overhead for the year and dividing by the total direct labor for the year (including principals' time on projects). *It is recommended that overhead be recalculated at least quarterly for budgeting and allocation purposes.* The report also shows a budget line item for overhead.

Nonreimbursable direct and reimbursable expenses

Nonreimbursable direct expenses are those cost (nonlabor) items which come directly out of your fee. Reimbursable expenses are pass-through items to which you may add a markup.

Table 12.5 illustrates the complete report incorporating direct and reimbursable expenses and total spent figures. The budget figures are taken from the project cost plan, while the current period direct and reimbursable expenses are from the project expense sheet. The variation between current period and project-to-date expenses represents

TABLE 12.5 Project Summary Report

Project name: City Hall alterations Project no.: 02792

Period: November 1–30, 1992

Compensation schedule: $14,500* maximum		Principal: Jones		Project manager: Doe	
		Direct Labor			
	Current period		Project to date		Budget
Phase	Hours	Dollars	Hours	Dollars	Hours	Dollars
SD (including predesign)	6	64	8	80	74	692
DD	4	48	4	48	40	280
CD	—	—	—	—	160	800
BN	—	—	—	—	10	120
CA	—	—	—	—	90	720
Total labor	10	112	12	128	374	2612

Overhead allocation (current factor: 152%)

Prior balance:	$ 24	
Current period:	170	
Project to date:	$194	3918

TABLE 12.5   Project Summary Report (*Continued*)

Nonreimbursable Direct Expenses			
	Current period, $	Project to date, $	Budget, $
Consultants	350	400	2,400
Travel	195	195	—
Entertainment	—	—	—
Printing	—	50	100
Other	—	—	100
Total nonreimbursable direct expenses	545	645	2,600
Reimbursable Expenses			
	Current period, $	Project to date, $	Budget, $
Consultants	200	400	2,000
Travel	—	50	300
Printing	25	25	500
Telephone	—	—	200
Other	—	—	—
Total reimbursable expenses	225	475	3,000
Total spent		$1442	$12,130

the previous month's expenses. The total spent figures are without profit, contingency and reimbursable markup. At the point where project-to-date total spent (currently $1442) exceeds the budget total spent ($12,130), profit and contingency would be used to complete the project. If this situation continues long enough (if over $14,500 in total is spent), the project would be losing money.

This report must be accurate and must be distributed on a timely basis to project managers (within 3 to 5 business days of the end of the period). Larger firms often require more data and add options including:

1. *Previous balance for both labor and expenses.*   This indicates what the project-to-date amounts were before addition of the current period data. In the example shown in Table 12.5, the previous balance for SD (schematic design) would be $80 − $64 = $16.

2. *Amount remaining to budget for each labor and expense item.*   This is computed by subtracting the project-to-date figures from the budget. In the example shown in Table 12.5, the amount remaining in the budget for SD would be

$$\$692 - \$80 = \$612$$

3. *Percent complete by phase.*   This input by project managers is based on their estimate of actual completion (not the amount of the budget spent).

4. *Percent of the budget spent.* This is calculated by comparing the project-to-date spent by item with the budget. In the example shown in Table 12.5, the percent of the budget spent for SD would be

$$\frac{\$80}{\$692} = 11.6\%$$

5. *Projected to completion by phase.* This assumes a linear flow of work. It is calculated by comparing the actual dollars (or hours) spent to date (by phase) with the actual percentage of completion (*not* the percent of the budget spent). In the example shown in Table 12.5, assume the actual percentage of completion is 9 percent, with $80 spent to date for SD. Hence, $80/9% = $889 at completion. Compare this number with the budget for SD of $692. If spending continues at the current rate you will be $197 behind the budget for this phase. The difficulty with this calculation is that it assumes a linear flow of work on a project (a fact that is rarely true). In some circumstances, however, it can be a valuable indicator.

6. *Effective labor rates by phase.* This compares the average hourly rate of all employees charging time to a phase with the average budgeted rate. In the example shown in Table 12.5 for SD, the average project-to-date rate of $10 ($80/8 hours) versus the budgeted rate of $9.35 (692/74 hours). Therefore, the firm is using more expensive people for SD than was originally budgeted. (Considering the 9 percent actual completion versus the 11.6 percent of the budget spent, these more expensive people are not as productive as they should be or the project is more complex than expected.)

Other options should be included on the report only if they are meaningful to those managing the projects and can be provided on a regular and timely basis. Computerization can be a great aid to a firm that already has a good manual system.

Chapter

13

Team/Client Management

Personnel Planning

Effective project management for small design firms requires tight control over personnel levels and utilization. The room for error is even less in small firms than in large, since the loss or gain of a single project can result in great over- or understaffing and thus seriously affect profitability. Clearly, hiring and firing staff as levels of work rise and fall seriously affects productivity and requires the constant training of new people. Maintaining staff at a planned level requires not only a consistent marketing effort, but also necessitates regular forecasting of present and future work loads.

Personnel planning is not an exact science. The key to its success is the regular discipline of preparing summary plans. A computer is not essential, but can help store and manipulate data. Human judgment is the most important element of an effective plan. The input to the plan should come primarily from those actually responsible for running projects. However, one individual must be responsible for putting data in a final form. The plan should be prepared at least monthly and reviewed and modified as needed each week. If the firm primarily handles very small projects, it may need to prepare a plan more frequently. It is not sufficient to mentally perform this planning exercise, since this does not permit a look far enough ahead to systematically and objectively examine work load.

Table 13.1 presents a suggested personnel planning format based on a firm of seven technical people. Note that this firm may actually have a total staff greater than seven, but for planning purposes only technical staff or full-time equivalents are used. Full-time equivalents are part-timers converted to fractions of regular staff based on a 40-hour

TABLE 13.1   Personnel Planning

FIRM: ABC Designs   Date: 12/92

Current personnel level: 7   Chargeable ratio: 0.85

Chargeable hours per work-month: 0.85 × 170 = 145
(thus 1015 available without overtime)

Project number	Work-hours (WH) to start	1st month	2d month	3d month	4th month	WH left
		A. In-House Projects				
9220	1400	200	200	250	250	500
9215	450	100	150	200		
9212	1100	200	200	200	200	300
9197	200	50	100	50		
9156	2000	300	400	400	500	400
9143	1000	100	300	400	100	100
Misc.	100			50		50
Subtotal	6250	950	1350	1550	1050	1350
		B. Probable Projects				
BD237	1500				150	1350
BD314	450				450	
BD256	1200					1200
BD295	300					300
Subtotal	3450				600	2850
× 75%	2588				450	2138
Grand total	8838	950	1350	1550	1500	3488
Equivalent employees		6.6	9.3	10.7	10.3	
Personnel						
Deficiency			2.3	3.7	3.3	
Surplus		0.4				

work week. Thus a 20-hour-a-week intern equals one-half of a full-time person. (The same calculation could be based on annual hours worked, using 2080 hours for an average work year without overtime.) If secretaries or others perform some technical work such as specification typing (and this is charged to projects), it may be desirable to factor them into full-time equivalents.

The chargeable rate is the percentage of time actually available to work on projects (without overtime). Twelve percent of total time is normally lost to vacation, sick leave, holidays, and personal time off. In addition, when calculating a chargeable rate for total staff, a significant amount of time is normally used for overhead-related items, reducing the overall firm chargeable rate to the range of 60 to 65 percent. The data for calculating chargeable ratios must come from historical records. The actual hours available per employee in a month is

4.25 forty-hour work weeks per month times the chargeable rate, or 145 hours available per person. For a seven-person staff, this results in 1015 hours available per month without overtime.

Analysis

In general, a personnel projection should be performed for the current month plus 3 additional months. Beyond a total of 4 months, the projection becomes inaccurate except for very large projects with a predictable work flow. The *Work-hours to start* column should reflect the project manager's estimate of actual work-hours required to complete the work. It should not simply be the work-hours remaining in the budget, unless by chance they are the same.

Section A, *In-House Projects,* reflects those projects currently under contract by the firm. Section B, *Probable Projects,* consists of those in the business development phase, including those in the negotiation process. The work-hours under *Probable Projects* are based on a preliminary scope evaluation or on a best guess. A weighting factor of 75 percent is applied to adjust for unforeseen changes. This weighting factor is for illustration only and should not be used by your firm.

Each month is totaled to arrive at the total number of hours required by all projects. This total is compared with the total available of 1015 to arrive at a total for equivalent employees. For example, in the first month, 950/145 = 6.6 employees are required, leaving a surplus of 0.4. As a result, the firm is properly staffed to complete its work without overtime. In the second month, the firm begins to be substantially short of staff (2.3), a condition requiring some adjustment.

Leveling work load

Tied to forecasting personnel requirements is the need to level work load to the available staff. This can be accomplished in several ways.

1. *Work overtime.* Although this is the obvious solution to short-term work increases, it can be counterproductive in the long run. Studies have shown that generally working 20 percent or more overtime for a sustained period (a month or more) can result in a significant drop in productivity. This will often negate any gains achieved by working more hours.

2. *Improve staff productivity.* A highly productive and motivated staff can readily deal with short-term work increases. A good working environment using tools such as overlay drafting and computer technology can greatly enhance productivity. In addition, keeping

staff motivated by providing bonuses and other incentives, as well as keeping them informed, can be very important.

3. *Control the timing of discretionary time off.* A regular personnel planning process can help predict work load bulges and slack periods, allowing appropriate scheduling of discretionary time. Vacations can be scheduled for slow periods and discretionary sick leave (for example, for elective surgery) can be anticipated and matched to work load.

4. *Hire/fire short-term staff.* Many firms hire some staff on a project or other short-term basis. This avoids the damaging psychology of the regular hire/fire approach by allowing short-termers to plan ahead and seek other, permanent employment while still drawing a regular salary. Some senior staff people who have left other firms prefer this approach in that they can seek their desired position while still working, even if it is at a reduced salary. Small firms often gain a great deal from having this expertise available for even a short while.

5. *Farm out work to other firms.* During very busy periods, it may be possible to shift some work to other noncompeting or friendly firms. This may be particularly useful for working drawings and is often advantageous for firms with temporary increases in work or where the additional staff cannot be located or hired in time.

6. *Find alternative activities for your staff.* When a firm's work load temporarily declines and it wishes to keep the staff together, alternatives are available. For example, many firms find marketing activities for their staff to perform. This might include the preparation of graphic materials, research, preparation of newspaper or magazine articles, etc. Alternatively, staff can be loaned to other firms that are busy or they may assist these busy firms by performing the work in your office.

The key to maintaining a firm's financial health is to control labor costs, and this requires a regular process of personnel planning. The plan is the basis by which a firm can take prompt action to increase or decrease needed staff.

Staff Management

The hallmark of a successful manager is the ability to effectively delegate assignments to other staff members. The growth of many design firms is inhibited by the inability of owners and managers to release the reins of control over to project and firm management. As a result, crisis management prevails as the overextended individual attempts to cope with a work overload and shifting priorities. Many engineers and architects have been slow to learn the skills of delegation. Often, those individuals who try to delegate do so improperly and are likely to be disappointed by the results. Other designers, either unable or unwilling to delegate, take the attitude that it takes more time to explain a task than to perform it oneself. In many successful and profitable companies, managers constantly find opportunities to train staff to handle delegated activities.

Techniques for proper delegation

Select the right task to delegate. Frequently, managers assign to subordinates tasks they find undesirable. As a result, they conduct little follow-up to see if the assignment is being correctly performed. Generally, a task should be delegated when the manager's time is more profitably spent in another activity. When selecting a task for delegation, evaluate the skill and experience of the individual receiving the assignment. If additional training is required, be prepared to devote the time and effort or do not delegate the task.

Repetitive tasks are ideal for delegation. Once an assignment has been given and the task learned, the manager is free to perform more important activities.

Select the right individual to perform the delegated task. Some tasks are delegated to individuals who find the assignment as uninteresting or unchallenging as the manager. As a result, they either postpone the task, perhaps to a crisis point, or simply delegate it to another (third) party. This last situation may result in the assignment being performed with inadequate supervision. The result may not be satisfactory to the original manager.

In other situations, the assignment may go to the most available individual without consideration of the skills required. Often, managers delegate tasks to their already overloaded secretaries or administrative assistants. As a result, proper attention cannot be given to the assignment. A successful manager tries to match assignments with skills and time availability. The manager will try to provide the necessary training if skills or experience are lacking. When an individual is overloaded with other work, the manager should assist in developing priorities and schedules.

Give the assignment correctly. There is a tendency on the part of many busy managers to simply delegate an assignment without providing adequate instruction. The result is that the individual receiving the assignment may waste time in doing the wrong task or may need to constantly ask questions. This defeats the original time-saving purpose of delegating the job. When an assignment is not given correctly or completely, the final result may be inadequate or may lack important information.

Many managers believe that the time taken to explain an assignment justifies their claim that they might as well do it themselves. This rationale fails to consider both the alternative-use value of their time and the educational benefit often gained by the individual to whom the assignment is given.

Set a time limit or deadline for the task.   It is a wise manager who sets achievable deadlines in advance of the real deadline. This allows time for corrective action, if necessary, and offers the opportunity to provide additional training to the individual receiving the assignment.

Failure to set a deadline implies that the assignment is either not important or is postponable. A deadline that fails to allow opportunity for corrective action can create a crisis situation, potentially damaging to the manager's immediate effectiveness.

Provide a review and control mechanism.   In delegating an assignment, it is vital to evaluate how well an individual is performing. This allows opportunity to ask questions, conduct training, and review performance. Review sessions also provide an excellent opportunity to take or direct corrective action.

Responsibility and Authority

One of the most difficult concepts for firm and project managers to implement is the equality of responsibility and authority. In many companies, project, marketing, and financial managers are assigned significant levels of responsibility. They are expected to meet budgets, deadlines, and targets, often without adequate authority to implement their decisions or to meet the needs of their tasks.

A common complaint in many small and midsized firms is that middle managers fail to take responsibility and initiative for their assignments. Often, this occurs either because responsibilities are not clearly defined or because responsibilities are delegated while authority is not. Where authority is delegated, the residual right to override middle-management decisions may remain with the principals, department heads, or other senior management. This problem is particularly apparent in firms where the founding principals or partners are still active and are accustomed to making all decisions. These entrepreneurs often feel the need to be highly involved in marketing, project decisions, and client meetings. As a result, they may inadvertently, or by habit, discourage the taking of responsibility.

Effectively delegating responsibility requires several steps:

1. Clarify and define exactly what each individual's responsibilities include. This requires writing a position description and developing a detailed outline of specific task assignments.

2. Train individuals in the use of tools and techniques necessary to meet their responsibilities. Some employees fail to assume responsibilities because they lack the necessary skills. This shortcoming might be in a technical area, but more often it is a lack of experience in communication skills, organizational techniques, or the management of people.

3. Allow individuals the opportunity to do tasks their own way. Unfortunately, some senior managers who have been doing a task a particular way have difficulty allowing subordinates to learn through their own errors or to develop their own way of doing things.

4. Use restraint in supervising the work of subordinates. Senior managers should teach, not dictate. They must also learn to encourage those with specific responsibilities to find their own solutions wherever possible. Second-guessing is a sure way to destroy a subordinate's decision-making ability. As a result, the subordinate will fail to take responsibility for assignments.

5. Delegate sufficient authority to perform the assignment. In general, to adequately perform tasks requires at least rough equality of responsibility and authority. Any significant imbalance in this equation will seriously handicap decision-making ability.

Keeping Clients

It is crucial for design firms to keep their clients. Many practices obtain the largest part of their work from repeat clients. One well-known financial industry observer has identified five keys to client retention:

1. *Respect.* Treat clients, whether institutional or individual, with respect. If you respect your clients, they will in turn respect you and your organization. Take the time to find out what they want.

Listen to what they have to say. And, give them what they need, not what you assume or think they want.

2. *Communication.*   Communication goes hand-in-hand with respect. Keeping everyone well-informed makes the team effort a reality. This includes all aspects of written and oral communication. From timely invoicing, monthly reports, periodic telephone calls, and personal visits, everything must be complete and well-done. Review clients' status on a regular basis. Contact them and ask for suggestions and comments. Determine if they need anything or if there are problem areas. Communicate both the good and bad news. It is always best that they hear the news from the source.

3. *Service.*   Emphasize to your staff that they must offer prompt and complete service to your clients. Research and implement controls and systems to ensure that clients are getting the best service you can give. This covers everything from telephone procedures to individualized attention from staff. Quick response to requests and immediate resolutions to problems is critical. Respond to telephone calls in a personalized manner with courtesy and intelligence.

4. *Satisfaction.*   A satisfied client translates into loyalty and referrals. The combination of respect, communication and service will make a client remain with you. Satisfaction also means coping with problems in a way that all parties achieve their objectives and you maintain your client. Communicate to your staff the necessity of quick resolution of problems. A problem should never become an issue, at which time it may be too late to avoid damaging your relationship with the client.

5. *Loyalty.*   Stand by your clients. Seek ways to offer your help, your resources and your abilities. Do your best to help them solve their problems and needs within their budget and time frame. Your efforts will be repaid with both client loyalty and with the positive image that is communicated to the entire industry.

Client Expectations

It is surprising how many design professionals fail to fully understand their clients' needs and wants. Many designers have little interest in learning about client priorities, methods of operation, or information needs. Some professionals are even condescending to clients. These designers think that they know what is best for the client, and they want no interference. Unfortunately, these designers forget whose project it actually is.

Every owner/client is different, and their needs and wants also vary. There are, however, some needs that are common to most owners.

A clear point of contact

Owners and designers are often moving in opposite directions on this subject. In recent years, there has been a trend toward encouraging owners to hire all consultants directly. This is a result in large measure to the liability insurance crisis which has increased premiums for those design firms that hire consultants for their client. Designers can also be found liable for the errors and omissions of consultants if they hire them. When a consultant is hired by the client, the prime designer's liability is lessened.

On the other hand, owners are looking for one party to be responsible and in charge of the project. As projects have become increasingly complex, this need has grown. The result has been the development of specialists to fill the gap left by engineers and architects. Construction managers are now assuming the responsibilities formerly held by many design firms. The result is a deterioration in the designer's role, scope of services, and authority.

A design firm's internal project management structure can also frustrate many owner/clients. Owners are looking for one individual to be in charge and responsible for their project. When they have a question or a problem, they must know whom to contact.

Unfortunately, many design firms operate on a crisis-management basis. Often, especially in smaller firms, principals try to run projects, bring in new work, and manage the firm. Rarely do they succeed in all of these activities. A departmentally organized firm can only make the situation worse. In these firms, an ever-changing series of individuals is responsible for the project during its various phases. As a result, there is no one consistent point of contact.

Most owners favor the matrix or strong project manager system of project delivery. In this system, the client knows who is in charge of the project and whom to contact. Nearly all experienced and sophisticated clients endorse this approach and most employ it in their own organizations.

Clients want to be kept informed

It is a common complaint among owners that their design firms fail to keep them adequately informed on a project's progress and the design options involved. Most feel that the matrix management system gives them the best opportunity to keep current on the project.

In addition to setting up a matrix management system, designers must develop reporting systems, meeting processes, and monitoring tools to keep clients informed. While it is true that some clients are slow to make decisions, it is important to keep them informed. Often, they are slow to make decisions because the designer has not kept them informed or neglects a situation until a crisis occurs.

Clients want good cost control

To some owners, designers seem to be unaware of the costs of design decisions. To many designers, some owners want more out of a facility than they are willing to pay for. While this dichotomy may never be resolved, firms that show a concern for construction cost at an early stage of the project are most appreciated by owners.

This situation is particularly acute for public-sector clients. Many of these agencies receive their funding through a fixed appropriation, and they find it very difficult to obtain additional funding to pay for increased construction costs.

Technical competence is paramount

Although many designers don't believe it, most owners are more concerned with technical competence and experience than they are with the designer's fee. Clearly, design fees are an issue to many clients. However, most owners repeatedly indicate that fees are not as important an issue as many designers believe. Many owners look for design firms with quality control programs. After all, your clients do not need injuries, delays, or lawsuits on their projects either.

Clients also want to be invoiced regularly. This is essential if they are to plan and manage their own cash flow. Many designers are slow at billing or fail to provide complete and accurate information. The result is delay in processing invoice and potential irritation to all parties.

14

Contract Management

Contract Types

The selection of the proper contract type can be of critical importance to the financial success of a project. Often, the contract negotiation phase is the most important stage in determining whether a project will be profitable. Design professionals generally have a particular contract type they prefer, and they should try to negotiate this type with their clients wherever possible. The following is a brief description of some of the most common contract types and the advantages and disadvantages of each.

Time and materials (hourly charges plus expenses)

This is a common type of contract, sometimes called "cost plus," where the scope of the work is not well-defined. The design professional works at a rate which includes direct salary cost, payroll burden expense (employee taxes and insurance), general and administrative overhead (all other indirect costs), and profit to arrive at an hourly billing rate times the number of hours worked. Project expenses are billed separately, often at a markup.

This type of contract arrangement guarantees a profit to the extent that design professionals can charge for all their hours. The disadvantage of this type of contract is that few clients are willing to give the design professional a blank check. As a result, these contracts are usually written to include a stated maximum amount. It is important for both parties to understand whether this maximum is an estimated amount or a figure that cannot be exceeded without prior approval by the client.

Lump sum

Contracts that provide for the design professional to perform a certain scope of work for a lump sum are widely used. This type of agreement affords protection to the client and gives design professionals a guaranteed sum for their work. Regardless of whether the work takes more or less time, the lump sum is paid, unless there are changes to the scope of the work. In this event, a new amount is agreed on.

Lump-sum contracts are effective for both parties so long as the design professional is experienced with the type of work required and can estimate costs correctly. It is important to include a contingency factor in the lump sum to protect the firm from the unexpected. Often, firms making extensive use of CADD prefer this type of contract because it allows them to use their system and possibly enhance profits.

Cost plus fixed fee

This type of contract is popular for government work and, in theory, should guarantee that costs are recovered and a fee or profit earned. Costs are determined by using a provisional overhead rate while the work is being performed. The actual overhead rate is then determined at the end of the contract or the close of the fiscal year in the case of contracts that extend beyond 1 year. Adjustments to the provisional overhead rate are made at that time.

A problem with cost plus fixed fee work in government contracting is that the government operates on an appropriations basis which ascribes certain costs to different projects. If the appropriation is used up, no further funds can be allocated to a project without considerable justification and paperwork, even if the reason for the extra funds can be explained and documented. As a result, the appropriation generally becomes the spending limit on that project. Therefore, if design professionals spend less than their estimated costs, they receive reimbursement only for their actual costs. However, if they spend more, the extra costs are not reimbursed and must be covered out of their fixed fee. In theory, design professionals are still entitled to the fixed fee even if their costs are less. However, in practice, this may raise the question of whether a scope change limited their involvement and therefore the full fixed fee may be in jeopardy. In addition to cost plus fixed fee there are variations to this contract type that provide for various incentive fee arrangements.

Multiplier times salary

This method is quite common for design contracts. The multiplier is a rate that covers payroll burden expense, general and administrative overhead, and a profit factor. It is figured by multiplying the individual's hourly salary rate times the hours worked to arrive at a billing amount for labor. Direct project expenses are billed at cost or at a markup.

The multiplier method is easy to use and assures that all costs are covered. The difference between the multiplier and the hourly rate used in time and materials contracts is that the latter often groups classes of employees together and bills them at an average hourly rate. A possible advantage of using average rates over a multiplier is that individual salaries are not disclosed. A disadvantage is that average rates quickly get out of date unless they are revised frequently as employees receive salary increases. This can create a situation where substantial losses occur on a project because of the variance between actual and planned hourly rates (see "Revealing Salary Information to Project Managers," Chap. 10).

Percentage of construction cost

Contracts based on a percentage of construction cost are still used by some firms. Their popularity is fading as both clients and design professionals recognize that these contracts bear no relationship to the cost of work or the amount of creativity required in a project. Nevertheless, many firms are able to achieve satisfactory results on percentage of construction cost contracts and willingly accept this arrangement.

Value of service

One type of contract that is difficult to price is based on the value of the service to the client. For example, engineers who save their clients considerable money through the design of an energy-efficient building are obviously worth more than the value of their time. Design professionals should consider the value of services in developing their pricing structure to the extent that this is possible in a competitive environment.

There are many variations on these standard contract types, and frequently more than one type will be used. For example, until the scope of work can be clearly defined, a firm may work on a time and materials basis. Then the contract will be converted to a lump sum or other basis for the remainder of the work.

Billing and Collection

Many design firms hinder the collection of accounts receivable even before signing a contract. They fail to ask the client fundamental questions concerning how they are to bill for services and how they are to be paid.

In most small firms, it is the principals or project managers who should be responsible for improving the accounts-receivable collection process. Unfortunately, they often do not consider regular billing and collection to be an important issue and only become concerned when the checkbook balance is low.

As a result, many designers pay insufficient attention to the billing and collection process prior to or just after the contract signing. Basic questions must be answered that later will improve the collection process:

1. *What is the client's payment cycle?* If, for example, the client regularly processes invoices on the 25th and the firm does not bill until the 30th, the invoice will be delayed at least 3 weeks until the client's next payment period.

2. *Does the client require a special billing form?* Failure to use the client's form will delay payment. In many situations, the design firm may not even be informed of this reason for delayed payment for several months, thus several invoices back up.

3. *Is an audit required on each invoice?* Some clients, on larger projects, will require an in-house audit of each invoice. Failure to anticipate and prepare for an audit will often delay processing of the invoice.

4. *Does the contract call for inclusion of supporting material?* For example, should copies of time sheets or vendor bills accompany each invoice? Failure to enclose this backup will not only delay the invoice, but will create additional work for the firm's support staff who must reassemble this material from files. Anticipating this need would allow for assembly of a billing copy during normal processing of these items.

5. *Who should receive the invoice?* Many clients, particularly on larger projects, separate the invoice approval and processing function from the normal project administration functions of their staff. Sending the invoice to the client's project manager, if not the approval authority, may significantly delay payment.

6. *What are the late payment penalties?* Before signing the contract, negotiate interest penalties for delayed payment. Many clients will agree to this after 30 days, and in the case of the U.S. government, federal agencies must pay interest on past-due accounts (over 30 days) if certain billing conditions are met.

7. *Whom should the client contact regarding questions on invoices?* It is usually best to have all questions addressed to the individual in charge of the project, who may need to consult with the bookkeeper and call the client back.

There are many other techniques to improve the collection part of the process. For example, a personal note from the project manager along with the invoice may help create the feeling of a personal obligation on the part of the client. This technique, however, will have little effect where the project administrative and approval individuals are different.

Regular follow-up on invoices is vital. The first contact should be made within a week to 10 days after mailing to ensure an invoice has arrived and to respond to any questions. Regularly prepare accounts receivable aging reports to keep informed as to the status of billings on projects.

Regular billing allows the client to perceive the firm as a business-like organization that expects to be paid on time. There is, however, no substitute for proper front-end planning and follow-through. Table 14.1 provides a suggested billing checklist form.

In situations where the design firm is unable to promptly collect accounts receivable, there are actions that must be taken. Many firms do not negotiate interest penalties for slow-paying clients. For most well-run businesses, this would seem an obvious precaution. Unfortunately, many design firm managers believe that, since interest may not be collectible, it is not worth charging. This argument is absurd, in that interest charges should be used as encouragement for prompt payment and thus becomes a device to stimulate client action. In addition, in litigation, where an interest rate is not stipulated in a contract, the court may dictate an interest rate. With fluctuating interest rates, the court-ordered rate may not be satisfactory to the design firm.

In a recent Birnberg & Associates survey of design firms, only one-third of firms regularly charged interest on delinquent accounts receivable. The most commonly charged amount was 1.5 percent per month, with the range being from 1 to 2 percent per month. Firms most commonly began charging interest after 30 days.

Scope Management

A major factor penalizing project profitability is ineffective scope management. This is the process by which a project manager has an in-depth knowledge of the contractual scope of a project and effectively monitors activities that deliver the promised services.

TABLE 14.1   Billing Checklist

Date prepared: _____
Project no.: _____ or change order no.: _____
Project name: _____
Client name and address: _____
Client contact for billing questions: _____
Professionals' contact for billing questions: _____
Send invoices to (include name and address): _____

Others to receive copies of invoices (include name and address): _____

_____

_____

General questions:
1. Client billing form required? ☐ Yes ☐ No (If yes, attach copy)
2. Backup required
   ☐ All vendor and consultant invoices? ☐ Yes ☐ No
   ☐ Vendors only? ☐ Yes ☐ No
   ☐ Consultants only ☐ Yes ☐ No
   ☐ Other:
3. Time sheet copies required? ☐ Yes ☐ No
4. Audit required? ☐ Yes ☐ No
5. Normal client invoice processing date(s): _____
6. Other: _____
Specific questions:
1. Fee basis:
   ☐ Multiple of direct salary expense   _____
   ☐ Multiple of direct personal expense   _____
   ☐ Professional fee plus expenses   _____
   ☐ Percentage of construction cost   _____
   ☐ Fixed amount   _____
   ☐ Hourly billing rates   _____
   ☐ Other (explain): _____
2. Maximum fee: $ _____
3. Reimbursable maximum (if any): $ _____
4. CADD billing method: _____
   ☐ Hourly CADD billing rate: $ _____
5. Errors and omissions project insurance amount to be invoiced: $ _____
6. Reimbursable markup percentages: _____ %
   a. All items equal? ☐ Yes ☐ No
   b. If different percentages to be used, list and include percentage used

   _____   _____

   _____   _____

7. Interest on delinquent receivables:
   a. Percentage per month: _____ %
   b. After how many days from the invoice date?: _____ days

Approved: _____ Approved: _____
Date: _____ Date: _____
          Client   Design Firm

Many practitioners complain that their clients "nickel and dime" them into insolvency. This occurs when seemingly minor client requests accumulate or expand until they significantly erode a designer's profits. In other cases, the designer is to blame. A poor job of evaluating the needs of the project during the negotiating stage can necessitate extensive work that was not anticipated.

Scope management is the process by which these activities and requests are controlled. No well-managed firm can afford not to have an effective scope management program in place. There are numerous steps required to implement this program:

1. Do an effective job of preplanning on every project. This requires detailed checklists of every possible project activity. Every design firm must have a complete and accessible database of cost and time records on past projects. This information is invaluable when analyzing a new project for potential pitfalls in the budgeting process and for comparisons with current budget and scope expectations.

2. A system must be in place to monitor costs and time on every project. It is inexcusable for even the smallest design firm to not have such a system in the office. Many personal-computer-based systems are now available for under $1000. Manual systems are simply too unwieldy, too slow, and often improperly designed to provide the needed information. A job cost reporting system must allow for coding and monitoring of changes to the basic scope of services. This is often done by providing for a separate project number under the base job number. All time and costs relative to the change are then charged to this separate number. These changes are not always generated by client request and may be caused by circumstances in the design office.

3. The individual who is in charge of the project within the design firm must know the scope in detail. In most offices, this person is the project manager. In small design firms, however, the principal or partners may assume this role. Unfortunately, these people may be stretched thin and may not properly monitor staff activities to ensure that they fall within the contractual scope.

4. Changes in the scope of services must be monitored. As mentioned before, an effective monitoring system must exist and be made available on a timely basis. It is an excellent policy to establish a separate system to record time and costs if there is any doubt whether the activity falls under the basic scope of services. Consolidating segregated information with the base project data is far easier than attempting to go back and separate it from the base job. Some firms even prepare budgets for these segregated change orders, although in many cases the full extent of the work required may not be known in advance.

5. Time sheet management is an essential activity if scope management is to be successful. With a proliferation of change order numbers to a base project, your staff may become confused. Questions will arise as to the actual project or change that they are to charge time to. A simple process to control this requires several steps.

- A summary sheet listing all projects and change orders open to time charges should be given to all staff members at the beginning of each time sheet period.
- Every project manager must be required to review and initial each employee's time sheet *before* it is entered into the computer. Of course, this applies only to those staff members working on the project manager's jobs.
- The computer system must provide project managers with a detailed list of time charges for each of their jobs and change orders. They must examine this information carefully.

This process must be taken very seriously. Your profit margin depends on the quality of your time sheet management. Principals are usually the worst offenders in not completing their time sheets. To be effective, the senior people must take the lead.

6. A communication system must be developed to inform all parties of requested or required changes to the basic scope of services. No matter what the source of the change, all affected individuals must be notified on a timely basis. In many firms, this is done either verbally (telephone, meetings, etc.) or by lengthy letters or memos. These are often ineffective and leave a great deal to misunderstanding. To be effective, this process must be documented, but in a quick and easy manner. Many firms develop a series of shorthand work authorization forms that fill this need and can be sent to consultants, clients, contractors, etc. Often, these forms become part of the contract between the owner and designer and may require the client's signature before any work is actually done.

7. Develop the ability to invoice separately for change orders. In many firms, small changes to the project scope are absorbed as a marketing cost. However, if care is not exercised, many of these seemingly small changes grow significantly and reduce your profits. Many of these may need to be discussed on a project-by-project basis.

Contract Change Orders

The process of managing project change orders should be a relatively simple one. Unfortunately, many firms fail to adequately prepare a system to cope with these change orders (changes to base project), extras (additions to basic scope), or out-of-scope items (those whose status is not yet resolved with the client). This failure may result in lost opportunities for additional compensation, client conflicts, and problems with outside consultants.

Several simple procedures must be established to manage the change order process. Many firms without adequate project control systems do not segregate time and expenses incurred on projects with extra or changed items. Well-managed firms have built into their job cost accounting systems the capability of segregating changes authorized by their clients or items that may require future discussion. Typically, a suffix is added to the base project number to designate these items.

Where the change is authorized by the client, and a fee agreed to, a budget separate from the base project should be established. A regular project monitoring process must be instituted so that the project manager receives a timely status report on project changes or extras. In situations where the manager believes an item to be beyond the basic project scope, a separate job cost accounting record must be established until the fee and scope status of this work is resolved with the client.

A general rule used by many firms is that if there is any doubt concerning the scope status of the work, a separate job cost accounting record is automatically established. In many cases, a seemingly minor change that might normally be provided as a courtesy to the client grows into a significant cost to the firm. By immediately segregating these costs, the information is available if the firm wishes to seek additional compensation from the client. Clearly, it is much easier to segregate these costs initially than it is to attempt to pull them out of consolidated records later.

To be successful in managing project change orders, there must be an individual in charge who thoroughly understands the basic scope of services. Where no one individual is in full charge of the project, many such items may simply be lumped into the basic project cost records. Obviously, this directly affects the base project budget and profit potential.

Communication

The most important aspect of successfully managing project change orders is effective communication. Clients, consultants, and staff must all be kept informed of the status of any items that are either authorized or open to future discussion and resolution.

Clients

In many situations, designers and clients disagree over whether a change item or extra was authorized and how much the firm is to be paid for its work. Clients may claim that they were "only thinking out loud" and never actually authorized the designer to do the work. They may also claim that they never agreed to pay any additional compensation to the design firm. In still other situations, the designer may feel that a requested change is too minor at present (it may grow!) to request additional compensation.

To document these situations and to inform their clients, some firms have developed shorthand forms generically called work authorization (WA) forms (see Table 14.2). Normally, the designer completes a WA form for any activity beyond the basic scope and sends it to the client as a matter of record or for signature. This provides notification and documentation at an early stage before extensive time and costs have been incurred. As a result, a detailed scope for the change can be established, fees determined (where necessary), method of payment outlined, schedules set, etc.

Consultants

Coordinating extras and change orders with outside consultants can be a difficult task. Since these items are not covered under the basic agreement with the consultant, questions as to scope, method of payment, amount of payment, and schedule will arise. Situations occur where the consultant proceeds with work possibly beyond that required by the client or prime design firm. Often, the amount billed by the consultant exceeds that paid to the prime design firm.

One common solution is the use of a consultant work authorization form similar in nature to that used with clients (see Table 14.3). This form is the consultant's authorization to do the work and covers fees, schedule, method of payment, etc.

Staff

For projects with numerous change orders or extras, problems arise in keeping the staff informed of proper time and expense charges. Without accurate input, the project job cost records will be much less useful. To reduce this problem, some firms distribute copies of the work authorization forms or a summary of all active change orders to key staff members. It is their responsibility to monitor the time charges of staff working for them.

Effective management of project change orders requires a system and the discipline to follow the procedures mandated by the system. It is important to keep separate records of all extras, change orders, and out-of-scope items. Without these records, the firm will lose opportunities to obtain compensation for all actual work done and will be likely to have lower profits.

TABLE 14.2   Work Authorization

Client:	Base job number: _____
Project description:	Charge time to: _____
Location of project:	Date issued: _____
Project title:	Initiated by: ___ Client
	☐ Reference:

Description of work to be performed:	Starting date: _____
	Est. compl. date: _____

Phase of Work:
____ 0 Design; prelim. and planning
____ 1 Working drawings
____ 2 Construction and shop drawings
____ _ Work order number
____ _ Special _____

Distribution (as checked):
Client contact:
____ Design
____ Architectural
____ Job Captain
____ Cost consultant
____ Specifications

Remarks:
____ Structural
____ Mechanical
____ Field superintendent
____ Consultant
X̲ President
X̲ Controller/business manager
X̲ Accounting
X̲ Main File
____ Other _____

Client's signature: _____   _____

Billing instructions: X̲   Project manager.
  Included in basic fee
____ Change and/or additional service   _____
____ Not determined   Authorized
____ Special
____ Maximum compensation,   X̲   Principal in charge:
    if any $ ___ .

_____

Project manager to provide complete   Authorized
  information and check applicable
  boxes, including appropriate distribution of copies.

TABLE 14.3   Consultant Work Authorization

Consultant:
Client:
Project title: Job no. _____
Estimated completion date: _____

Instructions: This agreement is subject to and governed by all the terms and condi-
                tions of our agreement dated _____ entered into by the un-
                dersigned unless modified in writing.
Scope of work:

Special provisions:

Fee (including the terms of payment):

Design Firm: _____	Consultant: _____
Signed: _____	Signed: _____
Date: _____	Date: _____

Project Administration

Filing project data

All projects generate huge amounts of paper with varying degrees of
value. Locating a particular item can be difficult since individuals often develop their own customized filing system. Although any system
will work better than no system at all, good systems have certain principles in common.

Appoint one person to be in charge of the filing system. Duplicate
files and duplicate copies in project files should be avoided. Sort data
into similar categories. Bind data into volumes and do not permit individual items to be separated from the group. Provide a sign-out system so that missing volumes can be located. Check frequently to be
sure the file is being kept up-to-date.

It is common for filing to be a free-time activity. Unfortunately, far
more time is lost looking for improperly filed information than is
spent in maintaining a properly planned file on a regular basis.

To make project files usable, they must be broken down into sections of manageable size. Any grouping larger than what can be
placed in a single folder is too large for efficiently locating specific information. The Uniform Construction Index (produced by the American Institute of Architects and possibly out of print as you read this)
outlines suggested subject headings for file divisions. This needs to be
supplemented by office experience. A file should not be subdivided

more than necessary to keep the number of subdivisions of manageable size. The volume of material accumulated on a previous, similar project is a good guide to the amount that is likely to be generated by a new project.

Avoid elaborate cross-indexing systems. Simple chronological sequencing is usually the best way to locate documents quickly, since most individuals searching a file usually have a general idea of the time a document was received or created.

Separate incoming from outgoing correspondence. Do not bother trying to file letters that answer questions raised by earlier correspondence with the earlier letter. Many letters are never answered directly, or answers to several letters may be included in a single response.

Incoming correspondence

All incoming correspondence should be routed to the person in charge of the project. Some mail may need to be rerouted to others on the project team. In most cases it is wise to make copies of the document and distribute the copies to persons listed on a standard distribution list. Circulating a single copy to several persons is rarely successful since the copy usually stays on the desk of the first to receive it. Distributing on a need-to-know basis can also be a problem because the person in charge may not recognize the importance of a document to another member of the team.

To reduce the need for copying long or bulky documents, a memo acknowledging receipt and indicating who has custody of the item can be circulated in lieu of the actual document. Zoning codes or soil boring reports, which may be important to several team members, are often handled in this manner. It is important that the original document be added to the permanent file as soon as possible to reduce the possibility of loss.

The purpose of distributing copies is to keep the project team informed. Since the original can always be consulted, recipients should only save those documents which they will be using regularly. Technical staff members generally have no need to maintain their own job files.

Outgoing correspondence

Many firms require the project manager to sign or review all outgoing correspondence. Even seemingly routine inquiries to manufacturers may violate office policy or client requests. A copy of all outgoing correspondence should be kept in a central project file and a separate chronological correspondence file may also be helpful. Copies should be distributed to team members in the same manner as incoming correspondence.

Interoffice/intraoffice memoranda

It is often convenient to distribute job information by memo. Administrative information of no interest to the client is an example. Like any document related to a job, it is subject to discovery (legal) proceedings in the event of lawsuits. As a result, judgment must be used when preparing memos. For example, an internal memo documenting a project decision might be used to find the design firm at fault in a professional liability suit.

Job notes

Many firms find it advantageous to keep a special type of memo to record the minutes of job meetings. Most projects involve many meetings with the owner, consultants, contractors, government agencies, and others. Often, decisions reached are not clearly understood by all parties. By circulating minutes to all participants, the writer, in a sense, controls the decision-making process. Months later, these minutes are invaluable for determining the understanding of the parties at the time of the meeting. If these memos are printed on colored paper and organized in a standard format, their importance will be emphasized and they will more likely be read and acted on.

Work authorizations

During the progress of a project, many alternatives, scenarios, budgets, and schedules are discussed by members of the project team. Because most people are eager to get on with the job, they often misunderstand the significance of these discussions and proceed to do work on the basis of preliminary assumptions. Frequently, clients do not follow through with written authorizations of work discussed. The team should expect and demand receipt of formal authorization before proceeding with work. (See tables earlier in this chapter.)

Telephone calls

The telephone is indispensable for communicating information and assisting in problem solving. It has the disadvantage of not providing documentation of decisions and discussions. Of course, you can tape-record telephone messages, but this tends to inhibit the free flow of information and may be illegal in some cases. A better technique is to record decisions reached by telephone immediately after completing a call. A telephone message pad available at each phone encourages people to record calls and decisions made. Such a message pad should be standard 8½ × 11 inches to be sure the document does not get lost in the files. This process can be invaluable if questions about a job arise at a later date.

Sales calls

Design professionals rely on salespeople to provide them with information on building materials. Salespeople regularly call on designers to obtain advance information on future sales prospects and to ensure that materials are used correctly. Designers should recognize the quid pro quo involved and govern their relationships with these salespeople accordingly.

Designers should maintain a healthy skepticism of anything not written in the manufacturer's published data to avoid being misled by sales enthusiasm. Most firms find it expedient to direct all salespeople to a single person (often the specifier). This is more efficient for the firm but sometimes deprives other staff of the educational value of the sales calls.

Manufacturer's assistance

Many complicated products or systems can only be described and specified with close collaboration between the designer and the manufacturer. Designers should be careful in these situations since this close collaboration can lead to an eroding of the designer-client relation. Clearly, the client's best interests are not always the same as those of the manufacturer, who is interested in making a sale. Particularly in publicly bid projects, the designer must carefully explain to the sales representative that the manufacturer's assistance cannot imply endorsement of a product at the expense of others. Even when carefully explained, bad feelings can result when a designer relies heavily on a manufacturer to prepare designs or specifications. Whenever possible, this practice should be avoided. Designers should employ a knowledgeable consultant or pay the manufacturer to design the system to avoid a potential conflict of interest.

Confidentiality

Designers work for their clients and must keep the best interests of the client in mind at all times. Most clients consider their projects to be somewhat confidential. It is important that the project manager have an understanding with the client on what information can be released to the public, to the industry, or used in the design firm's own marketing materials. Some owners take the somewhat unrealistic position that all information about the job is confidential and cannot be discussed with anyone outside the office.

Most clients have a somewhat elastic definition of confidentiality. Although they may not want the designer to release information to the media about the project, most clients recognize that firms must gather information from contractors and salespeople and provide them with data about the project. The best policy is to insist on staff confidentiality, but authorize the person in charge to use discretion on the release of information.

Dealing with consultants

Most projects employ consultants to perform certain tasks. The staff must understand the duties and limits of responsibility of the various consultants. Work authorizations should explain what is expected of the consultant. Schedules should realistically consider when the consultant can begin work and when it should be completed. In addition, adequate communication is essential. Job memos and correspondence should be routed to consultants to keep them informed on the progress of the project.

Checklists

A list of items to check before completion of a project can supplement memory and provide a useful record of matters considered. Checklists take many forms and can be used with varying degrees of formality. Many organizations have developed a standard printed list of activities to be performed on all projects. Unfortunately, checking such a list can become a perfunctionary task and may provide a false sense of security by giving the impression that items and activities not listed are unimportant. A comprehensive list by necessity includes so many inapplicable items that all items become diminished in importance in the user's mind. Some excellent checklists are published by Guidelines Publications (see Resources for more information). Masterspec specification sections contain excellent detailed checklists tailored to the specification titles actually being used on the project. *Checklists,* a volume of specialized checklists prepared by H. Leslie Simmons and published by John Wiley & Sons can also be helpful. (Again, see Resources for more information.)

Other standard documents can serve as useful checklists. A master specification table of contents, such as found in Masterformat, published by the Construction Specifications Institute (CSI), becomes a type of checklist in reminding the specifier of items that may be required by the project.

Probably the most useful checklists are the informal ones prepared by the user. By jotting down a list of items to check as the project proceeds, the user has a handy reminder of specific items which need to be resolved before the job is completed. Job memoranda can also be used as a checklist. Before a project is completed, review old memos and check off all items to be sure that commitments made have in fact been kept.

Check prints

As project teams grow, it is imperative that each member know what others are doing. Up-to-date check sets provide this communication. But check sets can be expensive not only in the cost of the set, but in the time lost while tracings are being collected and printed. There are ways to decrease the cost of check sets and increase their effectiveness. Provide fewer but better check sets. Bind sets with spring fasteners and replace only the sheets that have changed since the last printing. Have several members of the team share sets. Encourage users to note incorrect or out-of-date information on the set. When sheets are exchanged for newer ones, the team leader can review the notes and evaluate their significance. Saving old, marked sheets can provide an audit trail when errors are encountered.

Fax machines

The facsimile machine has become almost as common in design offices as the copy machine. It is a wonderful device for speeding operations, but it also rivals the copy machine and computers in producing an avalanche of paper. Communications formerly accomplished only by the telephone must now be documented with a faxed communication.

Like telephone calls, fax messages imply an urgency that forces a quick response. This works against orderly mail processing procedures and may result in communications not properly reviewed by the appropriate members of the project team. Many firms have a policy of following fax messages with a formal copy delivered by mail. This increases the paper blizzard and may result in a communication being answered more than once.

Many facsimile machines still use a thermal type paper that does not age well. As a result, the message must be copied before filing, and some of the efficiency of the facsimile process is thereby lost. Fax messages should be date-stamped on receipt and routed through the same distribution channels as regular mail to ensure proper communication and response.

Confidential documents should not be transmitted by fax. If a document is so important that it must be followed with a mailed copy it properly should not have been faxed in the first place.

15

Project
Cost Control

Project cost control has two aspects. First, there is the need to control internal costs. This requires careful monitoring of your expenditures against your fee budget. Second, there is the need to estimate and monitor the construction budget. Failure to adequately do this may result in exceeding the client's willingness or ability to pay for constructing the facility.

Controlling Internal Project Costs

Perhaps the most difficult task of a project manager is meeting the project fee budget. Staying within your design fee budget is a tough challenge for even the most experienced manager. The project manager should not be alone in meeting this challenge. Many factors affect the ability to meet the firm's goals.

The matrix management/strong project manager system has its weaknesses, but it does provide for an individual to manage and monitor the project from beginning to end. As noted in Chap. 13, to ensure its proper functioning, the matrix system must provide for an equality of responsibility and authority.

No project management system will function well without a capable staff. A high level of experience accompanied by individuals able to make quick and accurate decisions will go a long way to keeping you within your fee budget. The goal is to achieve effective decision making at the lowest effective level in your organization.

Many things occur before you sign a contract that can have a significant impact on your profit potential. Specialization in one or a few types of projects allows your staff to become knowledgeable in the particular needs and problems of those projects. Research and programming, materials, time, and problems can be reduced.

A poorly prepared scope of services can leave many questions unanswered. This may result in conflict with clients or require excessive unbilled change orders to meet the program. Poor scope determination can lead to inaccurately calculated fee budgets. The extra work or change orders required to overcome this problem can be very costly.

Some firms compound this error by failing to forward-price their work. Contracts that last over a long period of time (a year or more) or are likely to be delayed must have an inflation clause. Without this clause, overhead increases and staff raises can eat away at the profit margin built into your project multiplier.

Controlling the client

Many firms hurt their chances at controlling project costs by failing to adequately control the client. This failure covers a multitude of issues. Not adequately defining a scope of services leaves too many issues open for the client to challenge or make additional requests for unpaid services. A disciplined process of recording time and expenses related to change orders is essential. Many firm managers recognize that it is far easier to consolidate information than it is to segregate it after the fact.

Scheduling the client's input is essential to controlling costs. Failure to plan for this input can result in delays in decision making. A key to making a profit on a job is to keep it moving smoothly through your office. Any delays penalize the bottom line. A regular meeting process with your client allows not only better use of your time, but also can permit a decision-making forum. Project managers also have an obligation to keep their clients informed. Communication devices such as change order documentation, meeting minutes, and regular telephone calls help to inform clients, and they can contribute to controlling the client.

Information systems

Perhaps the most important tool needed by project managers is an information reporting system that allows monitoring of costs against the fee budget (See Chap. 12). This information should be prepared by computer. Many commercially available computer software packages can be obtained. Rarely should a firm seek to design its own software. Any claims that the commercial packages do not meet the particular record-keeping needs or method of doing business of your firm may indicate an incorrect approach on your part.

Most well-run firms today collect time sheets weekly. This improves the accuracy of information and allows more current updating of project status reports. Some firms even collect and post time daily. This allows an interactive process where the project manager can use a desktop terminal to check the current status of a project.

No information system is of value if the information collected is not accurate. As noted in Chap. 14, time sheets must be checked before posting. Some firms require staff to obtain a project manager's signature prior to submittal.

To control project costs, project managers must understand the information provided by status reports. And they must know how to take action on the basis of the information. If percentages of completions are used, they must be calculated and posted as accurately as possible.

Outside consultants must also be brought into the process of controlling project costs. If they fail to meet deadlines, if they arrive at incorrect or incomplete solutions, or if they do not segregate change order information, your efforts will be affected or delayed. Wherever possible, communication processes must be established to assist in working with your consultants.

If a project falls behind budget, prompt action must be taken. It is vital to catch problems as early as possible. This is especially true if your projects are of short duration, where any delays in obtaining status reports can prevent effective corrective action. Staff may need to be changed in order to quickly complete the work or to correct mistakes. Time schedules and budgets may need to be revised to reflect the reality of delays or budget slippage. And the scope of services must be reexamined to ensure that you are providing what you agreed to do.

Estimating and Controlling Construction Costs

Projects must be managed in a manner which allows for the control of all expenditures. The following examples of estimating construction costs are used with the help of data gathered and rules of thumb. When a quick estimate is required, these methods should serve adequately, but ultimately more definitive methods must be used.

1. From past projects, cost is divided by the gross building square footage to determine the cost per square foot. In order to determine the new building budget, the cost per square foot is multiplied by the gross square footage.

2. Another method similar to no. 1 above, but more specific, is to use past data gathered for individual building types.

3. A method that is more specific than no. 1 or no. 2 is to use past data pertaining to each trade to determine costs.

4. The method of determining cubic footage costs in lieu of square footage costs has its advantage in projects with large gross volume areas, such as theaters and auditoriums.

5. Other rules of thumb for quick estimation of project costs are cost per unit (material), cost per bed for hospitals, and per-student cost for educational facilities.

Various methods which offer more sophisticated results than the rule of thumb methods are available for use by the cost estimator. All of these methods depend on historical data, and, obviously, the more current and detailed the data are, the more reliable the estimate will be.

Some of the methods used are:

1. Building unit estimating (based on unit costs of material and labor)

2. Statistical and analytical estimating (based on trends, mathematics, and the use of graphs and an overwhelming amount of information input)

3. Quantity survey estimating (based on the determination of the quantity of materials and the amount of time needed to complete specific parts of the construction)

Some methods lend themselves to earlier phases of a project, while others are required when a more detailed, concise result is needed. The estimator must have several methods available and must be able to determine which method is most applicable to both the type of project and the particular phase of that project in which the estimate is required.

Most of the costs of labor and material information are acquired from suppliers, contractors, and all of the other price-determining sources where costs are initiated. This data may be presented directly to the estimator or by way of publications which assemble this data for the estimator who subscribes. (See Resources for more information.)

Many other publishers of periodicals and magazines offer various types of cost control system information. The estimator's good judgment is ultimately the determining factor as to whether or not the on-going generation of cost analysis is maintained as accurately as possible. The human factor is not replaceable. Human error, on the other hand, can be partly eliminated by the use of computers, which not only calculate costs and analyze results, but also store cost data for use in determining construction costs.

There are additional factors which cause cost differentials in building projects, and these factors must be considered. They are the elements of costs which are caused by economic situations, use costs, investment costs, financing costs, operations costs, maintenance costs, alteration and improvement costs, etc. These elements must be researched as well.

Additional estimating concepts

There are two additional aspects of project cost estimating to consider. These are life cycle costing analysis and value engineering.

Life cycle costing. Life cycle costing analysis is a technique involving as many as a dozen areas of analysis that are examined to determine their impact on the project in terms of:

1. Capital investment costs (front-end construction costs)
2. Financing costs, including the costs of equity, short- and long-term borrowing, etc.
3. Usage costs, including people and supplies to ensure functioning of the building program (this is the ongoing usage of the building, including staff, etc. over the life of the structure)
4. Operations cost for heating, cooling, utilities, etc. (staff, supplies, outside services, etc.)
5. Maintenance costs (staff, supplies, outside service, etc.)
6. Alteration and improvement costs such as tenant improvements and energy retrofitting
7. Repair and replacement costs
8. Lost revenue costs (the long-range costs of not building)
9. Denial-of-use costs resulting from delays from the establishment of need to initial occupancy

Life-cycle costing analysis is vital in that (according to one study), for a government-occupied office building over a 40-year period, the life-cycle costs were 92 percent for staff salaries (usage costs), 6 percent for maintenance and operations, and 2 percent for the capital costs of the building.

Value engineering. Value engineering is a process which identifies the general functional requirements of a building and evaluates design alternatives to satisfy these requirements on the basis of the initial construction cost of the structure and its expected maintenance and operational expense over its projected life span.

In essence, value engineering is a second look at design decisions to evaluate the balance between the most economical solution for one portion of the building against those decisions made for other parts (or systems) of the building. It involves an overview of all parts of the project and the evaluation of all implications of a design solution.

16

Quality Management

Few design firms engage in any regular or formal process of quality review. Some may spot-check or occasionally critique designs and/or technical decisions. Rarely do designers establish a formal quality assurance program. These programs are intended to develop checking procedures, checkpoints, and lines of communication; assign checking responsibilities to staff; and implement training programs and a wide range of other systems.

Under the pressure of meeting deadlines and maintaining budgets, most designers tend to minimize their quality assurance reviews or to ignore them altogether. Even more distressing is the lack of attention to the development of a program to improve the quality of the product being issued by the firm.

The focus on quality must permeate the entire practice. Quality management is far more than simply reviewing designs or drawings at various stages of completion. It must include not only a review of the product but also an examination of the method of operation and organization within the firm to develop designs, working drawings, and specifications.

Peer Review

One important resource that designers can call on to improve their quality is to make use of peer review programs. These are resources offered by most of the major design profession associations including NSPE, AIA, ACEC, and the Association of Engineering Firms Practicing in the Geosciences (commonly known as ASFE).

In May 1990, *Construction Specifier* magazine reported on the history, progress, goals, and costs of peer review programs. As the magazine noted, "The ACEC first examined the concept of peer review in 1977. ACEC based much of its program on the first peer review program ever created for design professionals, established in the late 1970's by the ASFE. Thirteen years later, five major organizations have endorsed the ACEC program, nearly 400 firms have been reviewed and several types of peer review have been created."

In a Birnberg & Associates survey of nearly 900 professionals representing approximately 500 firms, less than a dozen have undertaken peer reviews. Most were not even aware of the existence of peer review programs.

Why this lack of knowledge and participation? One reason may be the crisis management approach that prevails in many firms. Often bogged down in day-to-day project problems, many designers fail to examine alternatives to their current methods or to learn about programs that might help improve their quality.

A second reason may be the cost of peer review programs. According to the *Construction Specifier*, "The firm under review is billed for all review costs, including travel and lodging expenses incurred by the review team, administrative costs and daily honoraria. Some smaller firms find these costs prohibitive, but compared to the costs of hiring professional consultants, the price is small."

The benefits received for the costs of the review can be great. Clearly, if the firm implements the advice of the peer reviewers, the quality of designs and drawings can be greatly improved and profitability may be enhanced. In addition, several of the leading professional liability insurance carriers offer benefits for firms undertaking peer reviews. For example, the Design Professionals Insurance Company (DPIC) will reimburse its policy holders for the cost of a review up to $6000. Shand Morahan & Company offers premium credits of up to 5 percent to policy holders.

Components of a Peer Review

Firms that wish to undertake a peer review must select a review team from an extensive list of trained reviewers. All reviewers are registered professionals with at least 15 years' experience, including at least 5 years in company management. There is inherently no restriction on the discipline of the reviewers because their technical knowledge is not as important as their management experience.

In a typical review, the reviewers examine documents and interview selected staff from all levels in the firm. Reviews cover six areas, including overall management, professional development, project management, personnel/human resources, finance, and business development (marketing).

Firms wishing to take advantage of peer review programs must contact their appropriate professional society. You will be provided a list of qualified reviewers. Obviously, the scheduling of a review can be complicated and can take at least 3 months to plan for an on-site visit. The review itself can be conducted and completed quickly.

Peer Review: Help or Heartburn?

John Schlossman, FAIA

The concept of peer review is controversial in some respects. However, as designers become more vulnerable to claims, as projects become larger and more complex, as contracts become more constrictive and threatening, and as clients want more service in less time, designers should take a close look at the way their practices are functioning.

Chicago was among the first cities to establish a peer review program for architects and did so within the framework of the AIA chapter in 1981. A quality assurance task force was appointed as a means of monitoring firms in an effort to curtail rising insurance premiums. Cook County, of which Chicago is the major part, was especially hard hit with professional liability claims at that time. The task force had the following charges:

To increase understanding of the causes of design and building failure
To improve communication among architects and other contributors to the construction process regarding the causes and prevention of building failures
To elevate the quality of architectural services
To enhance the image of the architect as a professional able to meet the expectations of the client
To reduce the number of claims against architects
To reduce the cost of professional liability insurance
To reduce the incidence and severity of building failures and client dissatisfaction
To attract more architects into AIA membership

During 1981, several meetings were held to discuss various methods of attack, to report on issues, and to plan conferences. Peer review was mentioned as a possibility, and numerous questions arose. For example, what constitutes a peer review? Who will do the reviewing? Will the results be made known or kept confidential? How long does the review take? What positive or negative effect might this have on the firm's practice, now or in the future?

Initial reluctance was anticipated; however, under the tutelage of Chicago attorney Paul Lurie, a leading force in promoting peer review for design professionals, it was decided that a team of professionally related individuals would conduct the initial review as a pilot program. Through interviews and examination of sample documents and resource material, they would gain an overview of the management and operational processes of the firm. From this information, the team could assess whether a firm was operating in a businesslike fashion and performing work in a generally satisfactory manner. The team would then make suggestions on how the firm could improve and what methods should be considered. While general management and operational procedures were to be reviewed, financial management and technical documents were not.

In Chicago, the peer review team was composed of two or three architects and an attorney. A nominal fee was charged to cover the attorney's expenses and the expense of any clerical functions for preparation of the report. The firm could reject any reviewer it wished, for whatever reason. A letter of agreement for the review was signed by the firm and a declaration of confidentiality was signed by all reviewers. Results were kept strictly confidential; they were revealed only to the firm's managing principal. Reviewers received a preliminary copy for comment, which they subsequently destroyed. With small- and medium-sized firms, the review process took the better part of a day. A larger firm needed a second day.

Several important questions are addressed in peer review. Is the firm organized in an orderly manner to deliver work in an efficient way? Is there proper paperwork and documentation to keep projects on track and out of trouble? What is the firm doing to identify potential problems? Does the firm provide enough challenge, satisfaction, and opportunity for staff members? Are they the right personnel to perform the work?

Prior to a formal interview, a questionnaire is sent to the managing principal outlining areas to be covered and requesting that sample materials be available for reviewers, such as a set of working drawings, specifications including front-end documents, contract forms, project logs, personnel manuals, and miscellaneous data such as conference memoranda, records of telephone calls, shop drawings, and transmittals.

The reviewers interview personnel at all levels within the firm, beginning with the principals and including project managers, senior architects or engineers, specification writers, construction administrators, and other staff. Questions include: What methods are used to develop and produce documents? How are documents standardized? How is information filed and retrieved? What are the reporting procedures of individuals? How are personnel interviews and reviews conducted? The reviewers try to determine the spread of responsibility, personnel competence, and office organization.

Once the initial apprehension is overcome, the reviewers find that everyone wants to be involved. Staffs are genuinely interested in the process and are curious to know the results. At one firm, all employees requested an informal meeting with the reviewers at the end of the day for a general discussion. They were interested in speaking out and learning how to improve procedures. The review process illustrated to them that the firm's principals were interested in improving the firm.

After the report is issued, a meeting is held with the firm's principals and the reviewers to discuss the results. Six months later, a follow-up meeting is held with the reviewers to see if suggestions and recommendations have been implemented and to learn their effect on the firm's operations.

At my office, Loebl Schlossman & Hackl, we discovered while preparing for the review that some on our staff felt we did not comply with many of the items in question. However, after extensive discussions, we realized that we do many things informally, but are indeed well-organized. What the peer review process did was to raise our awareness level. While our office was among the first to be reviewed, peer review programs are continuing and many other firms have participated. In nearly every case, firms have seen the benefits of the peer review and have encouraged others to take advantage of the program.

Developing a Quality Assurance Program*

A quality assurance (QA) program must address the quality of all services undertaken by a firm. Why should a firm take the time and

---

*The material in this section was prepared by Jeff Orlove, AIA.

make the effort to have a quality assurance program when its staff is perceived to be doing a good job? This is especially true, since the time spent in quality assurance is essentially nonbillable. These are valid concerns. However, the benefits are clear and lay in four main areas:

1. *Reduced liability.* Despite the use of great care, people do make mistakes. Anything that can be done to prevent problems and reduce potential legal claims is definitely worthwhile.

2. *Improved schedules.* Standardized methods and procedures, and the more organized approaches that a QA program requires, usually make the work proceed faster, resulting in improved schedules.

3. *Fewer errors and omissions.* Standardized methods and procedures also result in fewer mistakes. Less experienced staff can use tried and tested information developed by more experienced staff people, resulting in fewer errors or omissions.

4. *Higher profits.* Performing work on a tighter schedule, producing work with fewer errors, preventing lawsuits, and cutting the time required to prepare a defense all result in higher profits.

A quality assurance program can also help in your marketing to existing and potential clients. The program can help assure clients that their projects will be done on time and with fewer errors.

A quality assurance program must include more than the construction document phase of a project. It should permeate all areas of a design practice. This includes business development, marketing, accounting, personnel, as well as all phases of project management. A well-managed office has each of these areas clearly defined, organized, and coordinated. This allows each staff member to concentrate on a particular area with the knowledge that other activities are being properly managed.

Steps in developing a QA program

Organization plan. The first step in developing a QA program is to create a clear and concise organization plan that delineates the various areas of the practice. It should also clarify who in the firm has the lead responsibility for each area and how key individuals delegate other activities. In smaller offices, one person may hold more than one position and it is extremely important to clarify roles.

The plan must take into consideration the strengths and weaknesses of various individuals and the needs of the firm. Both corporate and project responsibilities must be clearly identified.

Project manager system.   A system for producing projects from inception to completion should be designed. Specific projects should be organized around a project manager. The project manager is responsible for the schedule, scope of services, and fees for organizing the team responsible for producing the design and documentation for the project.

The project manager interfaces with design team members, the production and field teams, and the various project consultants. The PM has quality assurance responsibility for that specific project and is the only project team member who has knowledge of all aspects of the job. Whether a project is a large, complicated one or a small, simple one, the same basic project management system is used. The only variable lies in the number of team members assigned to a project. The project manager may not actually conduct a quality assurance review, but must plan for a review in the project budget and schedule and ensure that the appropriate reviews take place.

Quality assurance development.   Our firm, Solomon, Cordwell, Buenz, has a principal in charge of quality assurance for both corporate and project activities. This individual works with a project QA director and a corporate QA director. The project's quality assurance director develops standardized forms, formats, methods, and procedures to be used by the various project teams. The principal in charge and the quality assurance project director research those methods and procedures they believe would be most beneficial. They also distribute material to the staff and conduct meetings and seminars to disseminate information that will allow projects to be done accurately and on time.

The corporate director of quality assurance deals with similar standardization of forms, formats, methods, and procedures related to general operations. This part of the program includes development of a project control computer system for monitoring fee budgets for specific projects, computerization of the firm's accounting system, organization of management information systems (such as a project fee, performance, and cost database), creation and maintenance of a technical library for use by the staff, creation of a filing system for drawings, specifications, and completed project files, and development of a procedures manual for standardization of frequently performed tasks.

Lawyer as a team member.   A very important aspect of a quality assurance program is the concept that prevention is better than correction. Key staff members should be encouraged to consult with attorneys on what-if situations so that contract language can be inserted to eliminate problems. This can also help in the drafting of documentation letters to prevent a problem at a future date.

Our lawyers have helped develop standardized contract forms. An attorney can also assure designers in certain situations that a perceived problem is not of concern. This allows the designer to accommodate the client on certain business decisions without increasing liability. This often fosters greater client satisfaction.

Summary

Organization of staff is the key element in any quality assurance program. Clear responsibilities and the use of standardized forms, formats, methods, and procedures will yield the benefits of reduced liability, improved schedules, fewer errors, and higher profits. It is well worth the effort.

17

Using
the Computer

The advent of personal-computer-based graphics programs has put CADD in reach of even small design offices. CADD techniques often include parts of most other design and drafting techniques. It also has some unique qualities and formidable problems of its own.

Why CADD?

Offices purchase CADD systems for various reasons:

1. *Competition.* Prospective clients often consider computer graphics capability a measure of a firm's competence and require its use. The rationale is "Since everyone else is using a CADD system, we must too."

2. *Marketing.* Computer displays can be flashy and attract clients' attention. Some computer users consider buying a system simply for its promotional appeal.

3. *Production efficiency.* In some applications, CADD can provide startling increases in productivity.

4. *Improved accuracy.* The clarity of CADD-produced drawings is not as affected by the differences in drafting ability of the drafters producing the drawings. Because of the numerical precision of the computer and the semiautomatic dimensioning capability of computer graphics systems, dimensional accuracy is improved.

5. *Product uniformity.* The style of CADD-produced drawings is more consistent than the style of manually prepared drawings.

6. *Additional services.* Computer systems have capabilities which enable users to provide services that are not economical with manual systems.

Is CADD cost-effective?

Many users who have purchased computer graphics system have become disappointed when promised economies fail to materialize. While some applications can produce dramatic efficiencies, it requires careful management and skilled operators to make an overall improvement in productivity. Using computer graphics effectively changes the way all the work in the office is done. Real economies are related to how well the firm adjusts to the different way in which work is accomplished.

Evaluating the need

In their rush to sell, many hardware manufacturers, software vendors, and seminar sponsors are claiming that design firms using CADD systems are more productive and profitable than nonusers. The few surveys conducted on this subject have usually been sponsored by firms with a vested interest in showing a better performance on the part of CADD users.

Before accepting this sweeping generalization, design firm managers should evaluate several points:

1. The type of work that a firm does will significantly affect the benefits of a CADD system. For example, a firm with projects of a similar nature, where some repetition of details and layout is possible, will reap far greater benefits than will a firm whose client base is made up of varied and complex projects.

2. Profitability and productivity depend far more on management skill and organization than on the use of a CADD system. A well-managed firm without CADD capability will be far more productive and profitable than a poorly managed firm with CADD. *Well-managed* is not synonymous with using CADD.

3. CADD is a tool that is currently being used by a large percentage of design firms. But do not panic into buying CADD simply because self-serving individuals make dramatic claims. Think for yourself and evaluate how your firm can use CADD and how it will affect your staff and organization. Also, carefully examine the value of projects where the client demands that interested firms have a CADD capability. In some situations, clients demand or urge use of CADD without a willingness to fairly compensate a firm for its use.

4. For many firms, the interim period of establishing a CADD system

will be a time of lower profits and productivity. Hardware must be purchased, software obtained or written, staff trained and reorganized, and management processes developed. Unfortunately, this period may last several years until all of the proper components are in place and operating.

5. By now, most architects and engineers have discovered that productivity gains promised by vendors are overstated. If their estimates apply at all, they apply only to certain limited activities. Talk to your peers, vendors, and consultants to determine which activities offer the greatest possibility of gain.

6. Learn how to properly bill for CADD use. Failure to determine and negotiate proper charging methods will result in lower profitability if the alternative use of labor could have been billed at a greater rate or in greater quantities. Some clients expect that any savings made by the firm in using CADD should be passed along to them, while the firm may consider this savings a reward for doing the work more efficiently.

There is no doubt that CADD can be a valuable tool. Designers should, however, be highly skeptical of any claims or surveys that "prove" that CADD use automatically results in higher profits and productivity. There are simply too many variables to prove any such result.

Using CADD Effectively*

Before embarking on a CADD program, an office should carefully evaluate the character of the work it performs. The attitude of key people regarding the way they like to work and the interest of all the staff in a CADD system should be considered.

One of the keys to CADD efficiency is repetition. Any drawing task that is repetitious lends itself to machine production. It is not always easy to isolate those tasks that are repetitious. A multistory office building does not necessarily result in a lot of repetitive drafting because normally only typical floors are drawn. On the other hand, a one-story school may contain a great deal of graphic repetition. To a machine, repetition is not necessarily repetition of large objects, but can be repetition of items as small as hatch marks. An office that specializes in a limited number of building types is likely to find more repetition than an office that does a variety of building types.

---

*Pages 149 through the top of page 156 were prepared by Gene Montgomery, AIA.

Willingness to use CADD

Computer use requires changes in the way work is done. If the firm is unwilling to change and is efficient in the use of traditional methods, CADD may not be necessary. Too, if the staff does not understand proper use of the computer, the investment may not be efficient.

Often, the staff is more ready to tackle computers than is management. Unfortunately, computer graphics cannot be implemented entirely by junior staff. The changes induced by computer graphics span all aspects of office practice. Only by continuous active support of senior management can the procedural changes required to take advantage of the computer be made. Patience is also required. It takes a comparatively short time to learn to use computer graphics equipment. But it may take a long time to learn how to efficiently combine staff and computers.

CADD strategies*

Because of the organization required and the natural separation of drawing tasks from other activities, many design firms have set up separate computer graphics departments whose primary task is to run the machines. In some cases, CADD operators may not be design professionals and may not have had previous drawing experience. The department is geared to producing drawings based on design and analysis decisions made by others. Recent graduates may be required to spend a specific time as graphics terminal operators.

At the other extreme is an office that expects all its staff to know how to operate the equipment and use CADD whenever it is in the best interests of the project. There are, of course, many variations of these two opposing strategies. It is important to consider the implications of each strategy before devising a policy for an office.

The first strategy uses the professional drafter approach to office organization. Since there is a great deal to learn and master in the mechanics of computer graphics operation, it is believed more efficient to have the work done by computer graphics professionals. The department can be organized with its own hierarchy. Equipment operators may have only the type of training required to run the equipment. The department's role is to produce drawings.

This organization can lead to serious personnel problems. Since all work filters through them, operators may act like prima donnas. In addition, the department may become divorced from the project, with motivations separate from the best interests of the project. Moreover,

---

*This material also appears in a modified form in *New Directions in Architectural and Engineering Practice*, McGraw-Hill, New York, 1992.

full-time operation of graphics terminals may lead to operator fatigue and burnout. Professionals-in-training, frustrated with the lack of project involvement, may look for ways to escape the computer graphics department.

The most serious problem with this organization is its tendency to inhibit more productive use of the computer. If the operator's only purpose is to convert instructions to drawings, then the operator does not have the opportunity or motivation to take advantage of the more sophisticated use of the computer. If a computer graphics department is a separate profit center, then the motivation is to produce drawings as efficiently as possible, not to complete them in the most satisfactory manner. Professionals not directly involved with the computer do not learn the computer's capabilities. Delegation of operation of the terminals to a subprofessional department tends to devalue the desirability of operating or using the computer.

The strategy of teaching all professionals to use the system also has limitations. It takes time to learn the system and a certain amount of regular operation to develop and maintain skills. In addition, if everyone is expected to use the system as much as possible, it is likely that time conflicts will occur. Some types of graphics operations are very simple and repetitive. It is a waste of a professional's time to do them when a subprofessional can do them just as well.

On the other hand, great economies can be achieved when the decision maker actually prepares drawings. For an engineer to make a sketch, send it to an operator to enter into the computer, obtain a hard copy for checking, make corrections, send it back to the operator, and then go through the process all over again, is both time-consuming and expensive. This is especially true if the engineer could have taken a little extra time and completed the operation at the same time the initial sketch was made. Even greater economies are possible if the engineer can combine graphics operations with analytical operations.

Most firms devise a strategy somewhere between the two extremes discussed. Their goal is to gain the advantages without the disadvantages. Firms must be aware of several other potential problems:

Operational problems. Certain operational problems are endemic to computer graphics. While there are no quick fixes, awareness of potential problems is vital.

Operator turnover. It is costly and time-consuming to train operators. It is disastrous if they leave the firm shortly after the training is completed. This problem exists with all employees. Its causes and solutions are the same with computer graphics operators as with other employees.

Operator burnout. Working in front of a cathode-ray tube (CRT) for 8 hours is not the same as working at a drawing board. The machine has its own rhythms and demands which tend to hypnotize the operator. Regular rest periods are required and sometimes must be enforced. Operators must have time to participate in other office activities. Many offices limit time at the CRT to 6 hours a day. The other 2 hours are spent in preparation, review, and other office activities.

Poor morale among operators. This is evidenced by surliness, lack of cooperation, missed deadlines, resignations, etc. There are, of course, many reasons for this, but three problems unique to computer operators stand out:

1. Operators are aware of machine capabilities which they are unable to use because of the lack of knowledge of their supervisors.
2. Unrealistic schedules are established that result in excessive overtime. Computer graphics operators cannot work the amounts of overtime that young architects or engineers are often required to perform. Fatigued operators make mistakes that take more time to correct, leading to more fatigue and more errors, etc.
3. Machines are usually separated from the general work areas. Operators become divorced from other office activities and tend to develop an us-against-them mentality.

Machine breakdown. Computer graphics equipment is very reliable. However, breakdowns do occur. Redundancy of equipment is desirable to prevent the office from being paralyzed by equipment failure. Offices should develop contingency plans to deal with breakdowns. Cooperative arrangements with other offices to share equipment during emergencies is a possibility.

Certain kinds of machine failure can lead to loss of stored data. The loss of a disk may result in the loss of a great deal of data. While this is an infrequent occurrence, adequate backup storage is needed. Backup simply involves copying all data stored on a disk to an independent storage medium. Most systems provide an automatic backup of individual files to prevent loss by operator error. Do not confuse this with the need for backup of the entire system.

Disciplined routines by the system manager can ensure that adequate backup measures are used. A minimum backup program requires copying, each day, the work performed (files changed) during that day. In addition, all existing files should be copied at regular intervals—at least weekly. All backup files should be physically stored as far away from the computer as possible to guard against an accident that could destroy both the computer and the backup files.

Key Concepts

Efficient use of people, machines and capital is the goal in managing CADD projects. Several concepts are important:

1. The ability to accelerate a CADD project is related to the amount of equipment and number of trained operators available.
2. Many firms regularly mix manual drafting and CADD operations.
3. Plotting must be carefully planned and scheduled.
4. Intelligent personnel policies are more important than the type of equipment being used.

What Do CADD Systems Do?

Gene Montgomery, AIA

In its simplest form, a CADD system is nothing more than a rather expensive drawing board. Lines and circles and arcs and text are created by the drafter and placed in a specific location by the computer. At first, computer drafting techniques seem clumsy and slow compared with manual systems. On the other hand, pushing buttons is less complicated than the pencil-handling skills acquired by the expert drafter from years of training. This has led many firms to staff the machines with untrained drafters and then teach these people to produce drawings.

While this strategy works for some applications, it assumes the drafter's only skill is the mechanics of drawing. But machines do only what they are told. To draw a floor plan with a machine requires the same thought processes that a drafter performs when drawing manually. The machine can bisect lines, locate intersections or compute dimensions with great speed and accuracy. But it is the operator who still determines when to bisect the line. If the drafter doesn't know, the machine is not going to tell.

CADD equipment can do some tasks incredibly fast and with great precision. A drawing which took days to draw can be copied in seconds. A portion of a drawing can be mirrored or rotated or scaled differently and placed in another location almost instantaneously. These are powerful capabilities. It takes experience and forethought to know how to organize drawings in order to use these capabilities efficiently.

With the computer, you are not restrained by the size of the paper; composition can be completely rearranged in seconds; details can be revised beyond recognition with minor rearrangement. These qualities produce work rapidly. But they can also multiply mistakes. Good judgment, planning, and understanding of the results of actions are essential qualities of a computer graphics operator.

Computer graphics files do not contain lines and arcs. They are collections of numbers which locate the various entities in a coordinate system. Every entity has a coordinate associated with it and the file always "knows" exactly how far one entity is from another. All systems use this quality to produce semiautomatic dimensioning. With the computer, there is no such thing as a rough sketch.

All entities are located very precisely in space. With this capability, machine drawings begin to diverge from manual drawings. A line does not exist as a line on a piece of paper; it is a line that connects two unique points in space. The line knows where it is and can tell you exactly where it is any time you ask. The simplest computer graphics system has files that mimic manual drawings but also contain information not existing in manually prepared drawings.

More sophisticated computer graphic systems add information to the entity. A line can be told not only its exact position in space, but also what it is or represents. For example, a line may represent the centerline of a wall. Various types of information can be encoded into the drawing and, with the proper editing procedures, reported to the user in predetermined formats.

Entities in a computer not only can know what they represent, but they can also know they are members of a specific group. And the group may know information about itself independent of the sum of its parts. Drawings can become repositories of great amounts of information not directly related to the graphics. This file information can be edited and manipulated by drawing-editing techniques which may be more easily understood than the numeric manipulation of conventional computer files.

Properties of the file can be amplified and supplemented by software and peripheral devices that use the computer files. The file can be read and viewed on a CRT. The file can be plotted by a printing device and turned into a drawing, looking much like a conventional, manually produced drawing. If the computer file was prepared as a three-dimensional drawing, software can transform it to a perspective drawing. More sophisticated software can read the drawing, analyze the information associated with the entities, and reach conclusions based on that information. For example, information describing the construction of the exterior walls of a building, the windows, and their orientation can be encoded into the drawing. Software can then read this information and calculate the heat loss for the building.

Further along the path of sophistication is software that can change the graphics on the basis of embedded characteristics. For example, the computer can be told that all 3-foot-wide doors are now 3 feet, 4 inches wide and the software would change the graphics accordingly.

Despite the capabilities of even the simplest CADD system, most users seldom get past the first step of using the system as a substitute for manual drafting. The reasons for this are many:

1. All manufacturers strive to make their products user friendly, which means that they are easy to learn and use, and are tolerant of mistakes made by the user. There is a basic contradiction between tolerance of errors and the computer's innate precision. Computer language is an elaborate code with a very precise syntax. Each time error tolerance is built into the code, it becomes more complex. If the machine makes judgments about the meaning of the data entered, then potential errors are built into the data. If the machine asks for clarification, then additional time is required for data entry. The contradiction is usually resolved by requiring accurate data entry.

2. Graphic data is comparatively easy to check visually. If line A is too far from line B, it will appear in error and the distance can be measured and verified. But if line A is encoded to mean that it is the surface of a brick wall that is 8 feet high, then the data entry problem becomes more complex and the additional information is not visually apparent. To use the data for heat-loss cal-

culations, you must know where the other surface of the wall is, what the internal construction is, and whether the surface is an interior or an exterior surface. A person sees and understands this construction at a glance. A computer can understand it only if the data are entered completely and accurately. It is possible to teach the computer rules about how to resolve ambiguous or incomplete information. But to keep the rules manageable, a great deal of standardization is required.

3. Software that performs specific tasks, such as computing heat-loss calculations, has a comparatively small number of potential users. As a result, the cost of development becomes quite high. In addition, few engineers make their calculations in exactly the same way. A small market, a nonstandard process, and a variety of proprietary computer systems all conspire to make the cost of software to perform a task, which can be done quickly on a manual basis, relatively high. As a result, most users never get beyond using their machines for basic drawing work.

Changing Working Methods

Drawing by computer is obviously not the same as drawing manually. The time required to do a particular task is substantially different. The most efficient sequence for doing drawing tasks differs. This would not be much of a problem if a design office's major operation was drawing. But this is not the case. While staff may spend a lot of time working at a drawing board, much of that time is not spent actually drawing. An employee may draw 5 minutes and then spend an hour researching a problem, talking on the telephone or checking a shop drawing.

Staff cannot work in the same manner when using a graphics terminal. Because the cost of ownership is high, the equipment must be kept running as many hours a day as possible. Not everyone with a drawing board can or should be provided a graphics terminal. Time on the terminal must be scheduled. This requires greater organization of each user's time. This organization leads to a different way of doing work. Tasks must be more clearly defined before work on the terminal starts. Once terminal work begins, full attention must be concentrated on keeping up with (or waiting for) the machine. Drawing tasks are more clearly separated from design analysis.

Because nearly every staff member has a drawing board in the conventional office, everyone can draw to meet a deadline. In the computerized office it is not feasible to put more people on a job in order to finish it on time. Once the office becomes dependent on the machine, the computer controls the schedule.

It is not easy to browse through drawings stored in a computer file. Many people in a design office need only to quickly browse through the drawings. Managers, for example, may need only to rapidly look at the drawings to judge progress. The designers may be interested only in checking that a certain wall is finished in brick. The specifier is looking only to see what materials are being used.

For these individuals, conventional hard-copy drawings are easier to use than a CRT. Unfortunately, the biggest bottleneck in computer graphics equipment is the process that converts digital files to hard copy. It may take 30 minutes to plot a drawing with a pen plotter. Electrostatic plotters are faster, but more expensive. But no plotter offers the viewer the convenience of shuffling through a stack of drawings.

Superimposing a computer graphics system on a conventional office without planning for a drastic change in the way work is done is doomed to failure. As a result, changes in office practice are inevitable.

Billing Clients for CADD

Determining a fair billing rate for CADD use is critical. For many design firms, CADD offers the opportunity to produce construction documents more quickly and accurately. Naturally, these firms expect that more efficient completion of their work should be rewarded with higher profits.

However, many clients feel that much, if not all, of any cost savings should be passed along to them. As a result, conflicts and problems occur in determining the billing value of the CADD system. There are many approaches, including:

1. *Lump-sum project fee.* Negotiating a lump-sum fee for the entire project eliminates the need to establish a value for CADD use. This method allows the firm to recover its investment in a CADD system and permits the client to negotiate a fee believed to be equitable.

2. *Lump-sum phase fee.* For many firms, CADD systems are still used more as a drafting tool than as a design tool. As a result, major CADD use occurs primarily during the production or working drawing phase. Fees for all other project phases could be negotiated on a separate fee basis (such as time-card) while the production phase fee is established on a lump-sum or fixed-fee basis. Obviously, phase start and end points must be clearly defined and incorporated into the owner-consultant contract.

3. *Value pricing.* This method establishes a CADD billing rate based on its value to the client. Unfortunately, some clients are either unaware or unimpressed with the value gained when their engineer or architect uses CADD. Many firms seek to convince their clients of the value of faster and more accurate drawing, of the potential of examining more cost-saving options, and the value of maintaining documents on electronic media rather than paper. Some clients un-

derstand the value of electronic storage of their project and require its use.

4. *Billing as a reimbursable.* Although this method offers several possible alternatives, the most common method is to determine all actual costs that can be specifically identified as CADD-system-related. This would include, for example, amortization of equipment costs, remodeling expenses, financing costs, reasonable training costs, service contracts, software development and/or acquisition, related costs such as long distance or other telephone charges, supplies, etc. Staff time would be charged in the normal manner. Charges should not be made for office space (rent), utilities, or any other related costs (unless excessive) which would normally be incurred without CADD equipment. Obviously, if you are renting a separate office or expanding your current space specifically for the CADD system, then these costs would be included in the reimbursable calculation. Some firms also factor in a markup on CADD as they would any other reimbursable. Clearly, judgment must be used in determining an hourly rate when billing CADD as a reimbursable.

5. *Absorb CADD costs in overhead.* Some firms place all CADD costs in overhead (except direct operator time) and invoice the client by having these costs factored into the firm's multiplier. There are many disadvantages of this method. For example, it increases the firm's overhead rate (hence multiplier) to an unacceptably high level. This increase may make the firm uncompetitive. Another significant disadvantage is that the inclusion of CADD in overhead automatically spreads these costs over all projects. This occurs even on those projects where CADD isn't used. Lastly, by burying CADD costs in general overhead, the firm's management is unable to determine the true costs of the system.

6. *Establish a separate company.* To avoid many of the problems of negotiating with their clients a reasonable compensation for CADD use, some firms establish a separate CADD subsidiary. This permits treatment of the CADD service like any other outside consultant. Costs are then invoiced to the client as a reimbursable. Some firms establish this subsidiary as a profit center which then provides CADD services to other area design firms.

The best CADD billing method depends on an individual firm's system, costs, office procedures, and clients. Design firms are entitled to profit from the efficient use of automated systems. They must, however, be able to justify their pricing structure to their clients. Without this justification, firm managers may be forced to pass along a great deal of their savings to their clients.

Chapter

18

Project
Production Techniques

The term *production* is most often used to describe the preparation of contract or other documents. It is unfortunate that production is the commonly used term to describe these activities, because it implies a manufacturing process. *Communication* is a better term because it emphasizes the purpose of drawings. The purpose of all production techniques is to improve or make more efficient the communication process.

Planning

A design firm cannot design an efficient structure without advance planning. The builder of even the simplest structure needs a mental picture of the completed structure before beginning. Likewise, designers must not begin a set of plans and specifications without first deciding what instructions are needed and how they will be formulated.

In planning these instructions, consider:

1. What you are communicating rather than what the product should look like

2. Whether you have the time and resources to do the job the same way you did it last time

3. Problems or errors discovered in the last job

When preparing the project budget, make it understandable by analyzing it in as many ways as possible, such as:

- Number of hours required per person
- Number of hours per drawing to be produced

- Number of hours to be spent per calendar week
- Cost of time per task
- Tasks for each person working on the project

Only by relating the budget to actual people and calendar dates can the budget serve as a planning tool.

Enumerate the discrete tasks to be accomplished. Units of output such as numbers of drawings often do not consider the time required for special operations. If it is necessary to spend time conferring with a code official because of local conditions, that time is not available for other production-related tasks. Failure to plan for such non-production-related tasks (which are really communication activities) can seriously upset schedules and budgets.

Many offices relate time, cost, and schedule by using critical path charts and diagrams. By forcing the consideration of all factors simultaneously, a more realistic plan is developed.

Traditional Production

Traditionally, the only physical tools required to be an architect or engineer have been a pencil and paper, tee square and triangle, and a few other drawing accessories. Drawings were the primary means of communication, and each drawing was created entirely with pen or pencil. Organization was dictated by tradition or made up by adding more drawings as the project developed. Firms can still produce drawings in this manner, but there are various techniques that improve the process.

Graphic standards

A set of drawings has a style, a vocabulary of symbols, and a method of organization that becomes an important part of the information transmitted. Drafters, as a part of their education and early training, learn a customary set of graphic standards. Without a formal meeting, most offices develop an informal graphic standard over a period of time. This customary dialect, if it exists, is a valuable asset for an office because it is largely self-enforcing.

Most offices need to supplement this customary standard with a formal office graphic standard. New staff members can learn the office way of doing things more rapidly if they have a clearly stated standard to guide them. The act of writing down a standard requires an office to review what it is trying to communicate. Even when a strong consensus exists, an office can benefit from an occasional reevaluation of its ways of communicating.

Various groups have also promoted industrywide graphic standards with the idea that if all drawings used a universal language, users would better understand the drawings. It is unlikely, however, that an industrywide standard will ever become extensively used, since many offices prefer to use their own graphic standards.

Any standard sufficiently comprehensive to adequately guide the work of all offices would probably result in some offices doing more elaborate drawings than are necessary. A standard should be tailored to the work of the office and should strive to reduce unnecessary drawing. Many customary drawings contribute little to communicating the design, and many customary symbols require more time to draw than simpler ones. In an attempt to do a good job, most drafters over-embellish their drawings and produce more than are really necessary. Standards should emphasize the minimum amount of work to be done rather than the maximum amount. Preparing a simple but comprehensive set of office graphic standards and describing what the drawings should look like and how they should be organized is the first step in improving performance.

Mock-ups

Some project managers prepare mock-ups or minisets of documents that show what drawings will be placed on each sheet of the final documents. The mock-up is drawn to scale and enables sheet composition to be determined before time is spent preparing a full-size drawing. A copy of the miniset can be given to each member of the project team as a guide to the work to be done.

When prepared by an experienced project manager, mock-ups can save time. Inexperienced preparers tend to underestimate the number of drawings required and overestimate the space required for each drawing. Many people also have difficulty determining actual details required at the time the mock-up is created. But the attempt to locate and identify all required details produces a better selection of details to be drawn.

Standard details

All buildings are more alike than they are different. It follows that the details of construction are basically the same for most buildings. When all drawings are created with pen and pencil, much redrafting of the same detail occurs.

By developing sets of standard details, an office assures that the detail will be drawn the same way each time it is used. As a result, less checking is required. Time-proven rather than one-of-a-kind details result in better construction. Standard details also guide the drafting of unique details.

It takes time to generate a comprehensive set of standard details. Most offices find it more economical to cut out and collect copies of details from previous projects. Office collections of details can be supplemented by commercially available collections such as *Architect's Detail Library* by Fred Stitt (see Resources for more information). Many trade associations also publish carefully researched suggested details. By classifying and filing these standard details, an office can develop a rather comprehensive file of details in a short time. An indexing and filing system is essential. Loose-leaf binders provide the most convenient way to browse through collections of details. Similar details are placed in one binder, enabling a researcher to compare many variations of the same detail.

Some offices use the CSI Masterformat as a guide for organizing details. For example, window details would be filed under Section 8500. If the file became unmanageable, it would be separated into 8510 "Steel Windows," 8520 "Aluminum Windows," etc.

Since details are usually required to illustrate the connection of two or more primary materials, some find it more convenient to file details under broader headings, such as "Wall Systems," "Ceiling Systems," etc. Other systems use a key-word cross-index to locate precise details quickly.

Once prepared, a set of standard details can be used in various ways:

1. The detail can be traced onto a conventional drawing.

2. The detail can be photocopied onto sticky-back material and applied to a conventional drawing.

3. The detail can be photocopied onto clear acetate and the acetate taped to a tracing and either printed onto a sepia intermediate or photoreproduced onto a new drawing.

4. The detail can be collected into a volume of details which supplements the full-size drawings.

With all of their advantages, why are standard details not more widely used? Some possible reasons:

1. It takes a very carefully prepared detail to be used on another job without alterations. Most methods of reproducing standard details make altering them difficult.

2. It takes time to locate applicable details.

3. Users tend to discount the reliability of standard details. Too often the detail does not accurately portray all parts of the construction.

Sepia overlays

When several alternative designs must be prepared, many designers draw the fixed background elements (e.g., the site plan) and then make several sepia intermediate prints of the tracing. The alternative designs are then finished on the sepia prints, thus reducing the amount of repetitive drafting required. Sometimes the process can be extended by adding subcategories of fixed elements (e.g., alternative column spacings) on different sepia background drawings and then making another generation of sepias on which additional design work is drawn. This way, many schemes can be presented without redrawing background data. Of course, revising the sepia may take more time than was saved, if for some reason the background changes. Good-quality sepia prints are also required.

Scissors drafting

Many details have been drawn and printed in manufacturers' catalogs, reference books, and other drawings. One way of reducing drafting time is to copy these details with an office copier or just cut them out of the source document and tape them to a blank drawing sheet. A photo reproduction firm can then photograph the pasted-up sheet and print it on Mylar or other tracing medium. Additional information can be added in the conventional manner and then the photo reproduction can be printed along with the other tracings in the set.

A variation of this system is to prepare small drawings of repetitive plan elements and then make several photocopies of them. The photocopies can then be pasted up like the details previously described. Some designers object to the different drawing styles likely to occur when drawings are assembled from various sources. And the cost of the photodrawing must be deducted from the cost of the time saved.

Particularly suited for renovation work, photodrafting is similar to scissors drafting in that photographs are printed onto drafting film. Notes and additional details can be added to the photographs the same way they are added to hand-drawn documents. By using a perspective-correcting camera, distortions on the photo can be minimized.

Pin-bar overlays

Another technique relying heavily on photoreproduction services is pin-bar overlays. Mylar drafting film tracings are very rugged, dimensionally stable, and transparent, and can be stacked several layers deep. Drawings on different layers can be seen and printed as a single composite drawing. By placing different classes of drawings on different overlays, the same tracing can be used in several different composite drawings. For example, walls can be drawn on one overlay, ceiling plan on another, title block on a third, and architectural notes and titles on a fourth. By combining the first, third, and fourth overlays, an architectural floor plan is produced. By combining the first, second, and third, a ceiling plan is produced.

To keep the overlays in perfect registration, the sheets have holes punched in the borders which fit over a bar fitted with short pins. Hence, the name of the system. Overlays save drafting time, but even more important, they can improve coordination. In multidiscipline plans, a change in one plan is correctly transmitted to the composite drawing of all disciplines.

Many tracings are produced when the pin-bar system is used. Handling and storing the tracings can be expensive and confusing. Special instructions to the printer are required and errors in printing are frequent. As a result, reproduction costs are high and extra time for printing must be planned for. Nevertheless, the drafting efficiencies and improved coordination outweigh the disadvantages.

Details in specifications

Most details can be made to fit on an 8½- by 11-inch sheet of paper. If each detail is drawn on a separate piece of paper, problems of sheet composition are avoided. The same detail may be used on different jobs. Production often goes faster when the drafter can see drawings being completed more quickly.

Some firms collect details prepared in this manner and add them to their specification book or produce a separate volume of details. Detail books can make the use of large-scale drawings more convenient by reducing the paper handling required. Usually more details are produced if the small format is chosen. Some contractors dislike having details in a separate volume, since they can get separated from the full-size drawings. This results in users trying to proceed without reference to the detail book. However, it is often more convenient to use the separate detail book than to turn back and forth between large drawing sheets.

Freehand drawings

Most designers prepare freehand sketches which are later expanded into hard-line drawings. Often, these sketches are more informative and easier to understand than the more elaborate drawings issued as working drawings. By spending some extra time on the sketch, some designers are able to skip the entire hard-line drawing process.

Freehand drawings often more accurately portray the irregularities, misalignments, and inaccuracies of actual building conditions. Because they are drawn rapidly, they often show only the essential elements of the detail, omitting excessive information, and thus are easier to understand.

Some designers actually sketch over hard-line drawings in order to obtain the clarity of freehand drawings. Of course, not all drafters can do freehand drawings well. But a good freehand drafter can produce a great many drawings in a short time.

Computer word processor notes and schedules

Drawings contain many groups of notes and schedules that require hours of hand lettering to produce. Text can be produced by a computer word processor in a fraction of the time required to produce hand lettering. Since the text on drawings involves the distinct operations of assembling the information and then placing it on the drawing, this work can often be more economically produced by typing the data on a sticky-back appliqué and then placing it on the drawing.

Preprinted schedule formats

Standardization can be enforced by using preprinted schedule formats or preprinted drawings. Preprinted formats with blanks left to be completed by the drafter reduce the chance of forgetting vital information. Preprinted title sheets explaining the graphic standards used in the drawings discourage drafters from inventing new symbols and conventions.

Summary

The purpose of production activities is to communicate the design concept to others. Any technique that improves communication and reduces cost should be considered.

Time Management

Avoiding Crisis Management

Many designers continually complain about the lack of time in their lives. Crisis management in their practices makes their time management inefficient. Their families pay the price in the designer's absence because of job demands.

One important solution is the reorganization of the firm's internal operations into a more efficient system. Many small design firm principals attempt to manage projects day-to-day, besides managing the operation of their practices. Few individuals can handle both effectively.

Short of a total reorganization of the firm, there are many other ideas and approaches that designers can use to improve time management:

1. Control the number of people you come in contact with each day. This can be achieved in part by holding regularly scheduled meetings. This avoids ad hoc meetings. Encourage decision making within your firm at the lowest effective level. By preventing most decisions from being "kicked upstairs," bottlenecks are avoided and your time can be more effectively spent.

2. Try using a quiet hour in your office. The goal of this concept is to create a period of time each day for quiet office work that involves concentration. Many designers now achieve this by coming in very early in the morning, staying late at night or coming into the office on weekends. This strain on family life and on the individual can be lessened by using the quiet hour. Firms using this concept set aside an hour each day free of meetings, interruptions and telephone calls. The receptionist takes messages on all except emergency calls. Intraoffice calls are not permitted, and you cannot visit with anyone else in the office. Nearly all firms that use the quiet

hour eventually abandon its use simply because it is not enforced and individuals do not respect each other's time.

3. Improved delegation can improve time management. The hallmark of a successful manager is the ability to effectively delegate assignment to other staff members. Many engineers and architects have been slow to learn the skills of delegation. Often, those individuals who try to delegate do so improperly and are disappointed by the results. Other designers, either unable or unwilling to delegate, take the attitude that it takes you more time to explain a task than to perform it yourself. In many successful and profitable companies, managers constantly seek opportunities to train staff to handle delegated activities.

4. Managing meetings more effectively can improve your time management. Designers seem to love to hold meetings. This may be a result of their desire to reach decisions by consensus or simply because the need for meetings is inherent in the business. Whatever the reason, it is important to learn how to run an effective meeting.

Specific suggestions to improve your meetings include:

1. *Hold regularly scheduled meetings.*   Rather than deal with an endless series of ad hoc meetings, wherever possible defer discussion of topics to your next regularly scheduled meeting. Typically these include: weekly marketing meetings, project team meetings, biweekly firm management meetings, weekly project manager meetings, and weekly or biweekly client meetings.

2. *Prepare an agenda and stick with it.*   Distributing an agenda well in advance of a meeting serves as a reminder of its time and purpose, encourages advance preparation, and provides a framework for discussion. The agenda aids in preventing the meeting from going off on tangents.

3. *Apply effective time management techniques to your meetings.*   Start your meetings at the designated time even if several individuals are missing. Although a quick review may be necessary for those who are tardy, it is better to accomplish something than sit and wait for stragglers. In your minutes, list not only those present and absent, but also those who were late and by how long. (Some firms fine those who are late, but this technique is likely to be more effective for internal meetings rather than for those with clients.) Discourage small talk and extraneous conversation, since this disrupts the meeting and wastes time. Do not allow any interruptions for telephone calls, staff questions, etc., since these waste time and

disrupt the flow of the meeting. Always set a time limit for your meetings, and, wherever possible, stick with it by conveying a sense of urgency to the time scheduled.

4. *Use minutes and notes effectively.* The minutes not only record discussions, but also record what decisions were made and what actions are to be taken and by whom, set deadlines, and ensure that all attendees and interested parties have a complete and accurate transcript of the meeting. In order to ensure prompt action following your meeting, distribute what is known as *instant minutes*. These are nothing more than a photocopy of the minute-taker's notes. Without this immediate encouragement to actions, many individuals wait for the formal typed minutes to be distributed. This delay (often 1 to 2 weeks) may result in informal meetings to refresh memories, review decisions, etc. Formal minutes are important and should follow your instant minutes.

5. *Manage your meetings effectively.* Always have a chairperson. Make sure everyone comes to the meeting prepared by distributing the agenda well in advance and by calling everyone to review what is expected of them at the meeting. If it is obvious that the attendees are not prepared, immediately set a new date and promptly adjourn. At the beginning of your meeting, review the agenda, summarize the results of past meetings, and emphasize the time frame allotted. At the conclusion of the meeting, review key decisions, actions to be taken, and by whom, and due dates.

Other ideas

There are many other effective time management techniques. It is important to find the ones that work best for you. For example, a pocket calendar can be helpful in planning each day and future meetings. Make a list of things to do each morning and cross them off as they are accomplished. This gives you a measure of your progress during the day.

Telephone Time Management

We all need the telephone. It is our most effective communications tool and source of needed information. However, the telephone can be a major time waster and it can be disruptive to your work day. Business calls, solicitations, responses to your inquiries, etc., all interfere with the effective use of your time. Even a short call can disrupt your thought processes, causing a need to refocus on the task at hand. With some effort, you can make it less disruptive and more effective.

Suggestions

Use voice mail systems. In a great many cases, telephone calls are made to obtain an answer to a question or to respond to someone else's question. Often, you do not actually need to speak with the other party. Since receptionists and secretaries may be poor at recording and transmitting information, the human intermediary is not adequate.

The great advantage of voice mail (tape recorders) is the ability to give complete and specific information to the listener. This can be a tremendous time saver and can prevent misunderstandings and confusion. Unfortunately, some firms with voice mail systems only provide 30 to 60 seconds of recording time. Smart firms allow unrestricted time periods.

Voice mail also allows after hours access or communication when you are out of the office. Of course, voice mail equipment provides an excellent way to screen calls or to avoid constant interruptions while not missing an important call or information.

Many low-cost voice mail systems are available. The most common is the typical telephone answering machine. It is an essential time-saving tool.

Train your receptionist in proper telephone techniques. Many receptionists and secretaries cost you time when they should save you time. Few take a proper telephone message. A name, time, and return number is totally inadequate. They should try to assist the calling party and save you time by asking what the call concerns, can they be of assistance, when is the best time for you to return the call, etc. Secretaries must learn to judge what is an important call to you and which can be put off. You should tell them when you are expecting an important call and what action to take when it comes in.

Do not have your secretary place your calls for you. This is highly inconsiderate of the receiving party and actually can cost you time. Most people are offended by being put on hold by a secretary until the caller gets on the line because it wastes their time.

Keep your secretary and receptionist informed of upcoming meetings and other office activities. This allows them to suggest another individual to assist the caller in the event you are not available.

Batch your return of calls. If you wish to work uninterrupted during the day, have your receptionist or secretary take messages for most calls. Set aside the last hour of the day to return these calls. When working regionally or nationwide, this can also save on long-distance telephone rates (except in the Pacific time zone).

Leave complete messages. You should leave not only your name and telephone number, but the reason for your call, best time for you to be reached, and what information you are seeking (if any).

20

Project Closeout

After the punch lists have been completed and the final actions taken, the project manager remains an important part of ensuring client satisfaction. Regular follow-up with a telephone call or meeting will let the client know you are concerned about service and satisfaction.

Time and expense spent giving attention to problems should be immediate and may not be billable, but may need to be charged to marketing. The client should be kept informed of your firm's activities and should receive all relevant mailers. Remember, the client remains a client after the project is finished and deserves your continued contact and attention.

Project Data Retention

Once a design project has been completed, a decision must be made as to the fate of the vast amount of data and material collected during the project's life. No firm can or should save everything. Many of the materials that accumulate are redundant, are working or draft versions, or are progress reports. The "pack rat" firm that saves everything will soon be overwhelmed. A firm that discards nearly everything will soon find itself regretting the decision. Equally at risk is a firm that retains the wrong materials or one that fails to organize them in a useful form. Increasingly, firms are saving much of the needed data electronically. Not only does this save space, but many clients are now requiring their own copy of this electronically stored information.

Some materials must be retained. As-built drawings should be kept for as long as the building stands. Your firm may be the only source of these important documents. Future engineers, architects, and building owners will be saved much time and expense if they have these drawings available. The project specifications are also vital to enable others to review the material and equipment used.

For historically significant buildings, additional information such as preliminary design drafts may be retained. This will allow future historians and preservationists to consult documents that indicate the designer's thought processes. However, the determination of *historically significant* is for the future to decide, not the ego of the designer. One clue, though, is the original purpose of the building. Single-purpose buildings, especially for a branch of government or for a single corporate user, often have the greatest initial impact and the longest life span.

Legal Concerns

Usually, the single overriding factor in determining the retention of data is concern over the possibility of future lawsuits. Most states have statutes of limitations for the filing of legal actions in construction projects. In general, these statutes will dictate how long you should retain certain information. In most cases, 10 years will be adequate. Check the statutes in the states where you work.

Typically, materials retained because of legal concerns include a final set of drawings at the completion of each project phase. The owner-designer contract and amendments (change orders, etc.) must be retained permanently. Correspondence that could be used to pinpoint responsibility or a standard of care must be saved. Many attorneys would advise keeping all correspondence until the statute of limitations expires. In addition, job notes, diaries, and field inspection reports must be retained.

Management and Marketing Use

Aside from the legal and historic uses, the most important reason for reviewing and organizing project material lies in its subsequent management and marketing applications. Many engineers and architects are contacted by owners years after the original project completion. This can be the source of much additional billable work and requires ready access to past project data. Obviously, it is essential to save and organize critical information to allow for timely response to client needs.

Project Managers and Marketers

In many design firms, the project managers have the most complete and accurate files. Often, essential data never make their way to the main files of the firm. Project managers may leave the company, taking irreplaceable records with them. Even when they remain with the same firm, the information they have is rarely available to other project managers or to the marketing staff. If the main files have gaps, then much time is wasted seeking material, records, reports, etc. that should be readily available.

Your marketing staff has a continual need for historic data on projects. Not only must the appropriate information be retained, but it must be organized to allow for quick retrieval. Without this organization, a great deal of potentially productive time can be wasted searching for information on completed projects.

For example, many proposals require submission of information on past similar projects. This often includes fees, consultants used, owner's names and addresses, contractors and subcontractors involved, staff and project manager's names, etc. Some of this may be easily recalled on significant recent projects. Often this is not the case.

In an effort to organize and ensure comprehensive records, some firms have established completed project files. These provide a checklist of required information and centralize all essential historical material. (See Table 10.1 for a sample.) They are not a replacement for the firm's main files. The completed project file serves as a supplement, containing key data of value to other project managers and marketers.

Resources

Books and Manuals

Ballast, David Kent, *The Architect's Handbook*, Englewood Cliffs, N.J., Prentice-Hall, 1984.

Birnberg, Howard, *Financial Management for Small Design Firms*, Chicago, Birnberg & Associates, 1985.

Birnberg, Howard, *Small Design Firm Marketing Manual*, Chicago, Birnberg & Associates, 1983.

Birnberg, Howard, *Financial Performance Survey for Architectural and Engineering Firms*, Chicago, Birnberg & Associates, annual survey.

Birnberg, Howard, *Managing Growth and Change in Design Firms*, Chicago, Birnberg & Associates, 1990.

Birnberg, Howard, *Improving Productivity in Small Design Firms*, Chicago, Birnberg & Associates, 1990.

Birnberg, Howard, *New Directions in Architectural and Engineering Practice*, New York, McGraw-Hill, 1992.

Burstein, David M., and Frank A. Stasiowski, *Project Management for the Design Professional*, New York, Watson/Guptill, 1982.

Class, Robert A., and Robert E. Koehler, *Current Techniques in Architectural Practice*, Washington, D.C., The American Institute of Architects, 1976. (Out of print—contact University Microfilms, Ann Arbor, Mich.)

Eyerman, Thomas, *Financial Management Concepts and Techniques for the Architect*, Chicago, Skidmore, Owings & Merrill, 1973. (No longer available.)

Haviland, David, *Managing Architectural Projects: The Process*, Washington, D.C., The American Institute of Architects, 1981.

Haviland, David, *Managing Architectural Projects: The Effective Project Manager*, Washington, D.C., The American Institute of Architects, 1981.

Haviland, David, *Managing Architectural Projects: The Project Management Manual*, Washington, D.C., The American Institute of Architects, 1984.

Jones, Reginald L., and H. George Trentin, *Management Controls for Professional Firms*, New York, The American Management Association, 1968. (Out of print—contact University Microfilms, Ann Arbor, Mich.)

McReynolds, Charles M., *Human Resources Management for Design Firms*, Washington, D.C., American Consulting Engineers Council, 1987.

O'Brien, James J., *CPM in Construction Management*, 2d ed., New York, McGraw-Hill, 1982.

Piven, Peter A., FAIA, *Compensation Management: A Guideline for Small Firms*, Washington, D.C., The American Institute of Architects, 1982.

Simmons, H. Leslie, *The Specifications Writer's Book of Checklists and Forms*, New York, Wiley, 1986.

Stitt, Fred, *Systems Drafting*, New York, McGraw-Hill, 1981.

Stitt, Fred, *Systems Graphics*, New York, McGraw-Hill, 1983.

(page 178) Resources

Stitt, Fred, *The Guidelines Systems Management Manual Series* (five volumes), Orinda, Calif., Guidelines Publications, 1982–1983.
Stitt, Fred, *Architect's Detail Library*, New York, Van Nostrand Reinhold, 1991.
Woodward, Cynthia, *Human Resources Management for Design Professionals*, Washington, D.C., The American Institute of Architects, 1990.
The Federal Client, Washington, D.C., American Consulting Engineers Council, 1983. (No longer in print.)
A Guide to the Procurement of Architectural and Engineering Services, Washington, D.C., American Consulting Engineers Council, 1979. (No longer in print.)
Compensation Guidelines for Architectural and Engineering Services, Washington, D.C., The American Institute of Architects, 1978.
Architecture Factbook, Washington, D.C., The American Institute of Architects, biennial report.
AIA Handbook, Washington, D.C., The American Institute of Architects, current edition.
Guide to In-House Loss Prevention Programs, Silver Spring, Md., Association of Engineering Firms Practicing in the Geosciences (ASFE), 1983.
Project Management Survey for Design Firms, Chicago, Association for Project Managers, annual survey.
Guidelines for Development of Architect/Engineer Quality Control Manual, Washington, D.C., National Society of Professional Engineers—Professional Engineers in Private Practice, 1980.

Other Resources

American Society for Personnel Administration (ASPA), 606 North Washington St., Alexandria, Va. 22314; (703) 548-3440.
American Society for Training and Development (ASTD), 1630 Duke St., P.O. Box 1443, Alexandria, Va. 22313; (703) 683-8100.
Association for Project Managers in the Design Professions, 1227 West Wrightwood Ave., Chicago, 60614; (312) 472-1777.
Construction Specifications Institute, 601 Madison St., Alexandria, Va. 22314; (703) 684-0300.
Design and Construction Quality Institute, 1015 15th St., N.W., Washington, D.C. 20005; (202) 347-7474.
The Guidelines Letter, Guidelines Publications, P.O. Box 456, Orinda, Calif. 94563; (415) 254-0639.
The Profit Center (newsletter), Birnberg & Associates, 1227 West Wrightwood Ave., Chicago, 60614; (312) 664-2300.
Master Systems, The American Institute of Architects, 1735 New York Ave., N.W., Washington, D.C. 20006; (202) 626-7300.
University of Wisconsin—Extension Engineering, 432 North Lake St., Madison, Wis. 53706; (608) 262-2061.

Estimating Publications

Building Construction Cost Data, Robert Snow Means, Duxbury, Mass.
Berger Building Cost File, Van Nostrand Reinhold, New York.
Design Cost File, Van Nostrand Reinhold, New York.

Selected List of Computer Software for Design Firm Project Management and Financial Accounting

ACCI Business Systems
12707 North Freeway, No. 140
Houston, Texas 77060
(713) 872-4134
Contact: Paul Pamer

Harper and Shuman, Inc.
68 Moulton St.
Cambridge, Mass. 02138
(617) 492-4410
Contact: Bernie Buelow

Micro Mode, Inc.
4006 Mt. Laurel Dr.
San Antonio, Texas 78240
(512) 341-2205
Contact: Bill Henderson

Semaphore, Inc.
3 East 28th St., 11th Floor
New York, N.Y. 10016
(212) 545-7300
Contact: David Clark

Timberline Systems, Inc.
9405 Gemini
Beaverton, Ore. 97005
(503) 626-6775
Contact: Angie Hammond

Wind-2, Inc.
1901 Sharp Point Dr., No. A
Fort Collins, Colo. 80525
(303) 482-7145
Contact: LeAnn Nowak

For Macintosh:

Clerk of the Works (Samsara)
7905 Selle Road
Sand Point, Idaho 83864
(208)263-3543
Contact: Nancy Gerth

Index

Accounts receivable, 57, 117–120
American Consulting Engineers Council (ACEC), 41, 139, 140
American Institute of Architects (AIA), 35, 36, 39, 46, 59, 60, 72, 74, 75, 77, 126, 139
  Intern Development Program, 46
Association of Engineering Firms Practicing in the Geosciences (ASFE), 139
Association for Project Managers (APM), 17, 27, 34
Attorneys, 141, 144
Authority, 6, 11–13, 21, 31, 33, 110, 111, 133
Authorization forms, general, 36

Bevis, Douglas A., 50
Billing and collection, 24, 28, 36, 57, 63, 80, 114, 117–119, 120, 124, 125, 149, 156–157
Birnberg & Associates, 49, 119, 140
Budgets, 12, 26, 27, 33, 35, 36, 41, 45, 71, 99, 121, 134, 159
Budgeting, 19, 33, 36, 38, 41, 71–84

CADD (see Computer-aided design and drafting)
Career tracks, 22
Change orders, 4, 24, 27, 62, 69, 121, 122–126, 134, 174
Characteristics of PMs, 18
Chargeable rates, 50, 51, 53, 56, 106
Checklists, 4, 27, 35, 36, 59, 121, 130–131
Check prints, 131
Clients, 19, 23–28, 31, 32, 35, 36, 73, 75, 80, 84, 111–115, 117–120, 122, 123, 125, 129, 134
Closeout, 27, 28, 35, 36, 73, 173–175
Commerce Business Daily (CBD), 66–69
Communications, 6, 24, 35–37, 44, 112, 123–126, 127–129, 130, 159, 165, 169
Compensation guidelines, 59, 60, 72, 74, 75

Completed projects, 73, 173–175
Computer-aided design and drafting (CADD), 22, 39, 45, 56, 62, 116, 147–157
  billing for, 120, 156, 157
Computers, 86, 99, 121, 134, 165, 173, 179
Construction Administration, 27, 61, 76, 79, 81, 83, 84
  budgeting for, 76, 79, 81, 83, 84
  (See also Site observation)
Construction costs, 116, 135–137
Construction Specifications Institute (CSI), 131, 162
Consultants, 27, 28, 35, 36, 51, 52, 57, 73, 76, 81, 83, 84, 113, 120, 122, 124–126, 129, 130, 175
  selecting and evaluating, 61–63
Continued contract, 23, 26
Contractors, 37, 128, 175
Contracts, 36, 37, 61, 62, 69, 115–132, 134, 174
Costing/project costs, 73, 78, 83, 84, 114, 133–138
Crisis management, 13, 109, 167
Critical path method, 86–93

Decision making, 13, 19
Delegation, 11, 19, 21, 38, 108–110, 151, 168
Departments, 10–13, 113, 150, 151
Direct personnel expense, 56, 77, 78

Estimating, 19, 135–137

Fax machines, 131, 132
Federal Acquisition Regulations (FAR), 65–67
Federal work, 65–69, 116, 118
Fee determination, 23, 28, 71–84, 92
Fees, 33, 57, 69, 71, 73, 78, 82, 114, 133, 144, 175
Filing, 36, 126

Time management, 31, 167–172
Time sheets, 99, 120, 122, 134
Tools, 31
Total revenues/fees, 52
Training, 20, 22, 25, 27, 30, 32, 34,
   37–46, 157, 170
   budget, 45
Turnover, 17

Universities, 42, 45
University of Wisconsin, 38, 39, 42

Value engineering, 137, 138
Vendors, 28, 36

Work authorizations, 124, 128, 130
Writing and speaking, 37, 38, 40

ABOUT THE AUTHOR

Howard G. Birnberg is an architect by training and
principal consultant at Birnberg & Associates, Chicago,
Illinois, specializing in helping design firms with
long-range planning, marketing, and financial and project
management. He has served as an advisor to the American
Institute of Architects and the Pennsylvania State
University on the development of self-assessment systems
in project administration, and is executive director of the
Association for Project Managers in the Design Professions.
Mr. Birnberg is publisher of the professional newsletter,
The Profit Center, editor of *New Directions in Architectural
and Engineering Practice*, also published by McGraw-Hill,
and author of ten manuals on design firm practice.